# FADS

# America's Crazes,

ILLUSTRATED WITH PHOTOGRAPHS FROM THE ARCHIVES OF WIDE WORLD, NEW YORK.

**THOMAS Y. CROWELL COMPANY**  ESTABLISHED 1834   NEW YORK

# FADS

# Fevers & Fancies

## From the 1890's to the 1970's

## by Peter L. Skolnik

### with Laura Torbet & Nikki Smith

DESIGNED BY JUDITH WORACEK

Manufactured in the United States of America

**Library of Congress Cataloging in Publication Data**
Skolnik, Peter L
    Fads.

    1. United States—Social life and customs—
20th century—Miscellanea. I. Torbet, Laura,
joint author.   II.    Smith, Nikki, joint author.
III.    Title.
E169.S625      309.1′73′09      77-886
ISBN 0-690-01215-2
ISBN 0-690-01216-0 pbk.

1  2  3  4  5  6  7  8  9  10

This one's for Francis

## ACKNOWLEDGMENTS

The authors wish to thank Fred Canty of Wide World Photos, Robert Koretz, and Foote Cone & Belding. We are especially grateful to Rolf Meyersohn for his insights and observations.

# Contents

*Before he got religion, Billy Sunday was a right fielder for the Chicago White Stockings. Above, he winds up to zing the devil and the bootleggers, demonstrating the sporty style that had just made the temperance movement more than a funny fad.*

# Beginnings

"The passion we feel for our fads is as strong as patriotism, or mother love." So says Rolf Meyersohn, one of the few sociologists who has done any concentrated thinking about the bizarre phenomena we call fads. That passion, he continues, "is an authentic feeling, a real feeling, something to be taken seriously—even though the thing itself may seem trivial. And we are not in a position, you or I, to judge."

We do judge, of course, all of us. We have traditionally tossed off the word "fad" to describe either behavior that we thought of as silly—like goldfish swallowing—or novelties that we assumed, sometimes with collective nearsightedness, wouldn't last. In 1900, for instance, in two classic examples of national myopia, we called cars and movies fads, and with the use of that label demonstrated our failure to recognize the potential of carriages without horses and pictures that moved by themselves.

But the term "fad" has not been restricted to the apparently frivolous. It has also identified what some conceived of as a threat. At the turn-of-the-century we called various social and political movements of the day fads: temperance for one; women's suffrage for another. Sometimes it is only in retrospect, with the knowledge that the threat has passed, that we can reflect on serious national preoccupations and, with considerable relief, label them fads. Thus, in 1971, Stewart Alsop, writing in *Newsweek*, looked back at the 1950's and mused that Joe McCarthy was in his way a fad, too.

*From an early mail-order catalogue.*

*McCarthy and aides in powwow formation, April 1954.*

Silly or serious—goldfish swallowing or McCarthyism—most of our national fevers have eventually passed. Some of them, like Monopoly and pizza pie, have entered the mainstream of American culture; and others, from tattooing to raccoon coats, have dropped from sight only to resurface years later, attracting a new generation of enthusiasts who often don't realize they're on a return trip. But it's a rare citizen who has never been caught up in the frenzied whirl of a new craze. We are a nation of faddists.

We wear fads and eat fads, play at fads and go to fad events. In the 1960's we flocked to "happenings"; at the turn-of-the-century, it was Chautauquas. "The most American thing in America," Teddy Roosevelt called them, and over the years millions of us wandered into the big tents at the edge of town to hear the elocutionists recite wholesome poetry, the evangelists proclaim the Word, and the ukeleles twang a faddish Hawaiian melody our way.

Doctors are faddists, though they will blanch if you say so. The subject of a classic study conducted in the 1950's of how groups arrive at opinions and, by extension, fads, the medical men of Peoria, Illinois, were questioned to determine the rationale behind their adoption of a certain antibiotic. The drug had become popular in other cities and then, one by one, the doctors in Peoria had begun prescribing it—but prescribing it, as pharmacy records were to verify, in a certain pattern.

The most prestigious doctors didn't prescribe the antibiotic first. That adventure was left to those who occupied what was deter-

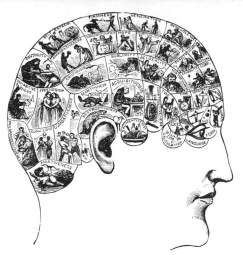

*Fads, funny and not so funny. In the 1800's the phrenology fad had us applying fingertips to skulls in a vain attempt to read our souls. Just after the turn of the century, music and literature came to town in a Chautauqua tent, and we sent away for Chautauqua desks and lamps. solid proof that culture hadn't passed us by. In the 1950's Joe McCarthy hawked fear. We bought it.*

*From an 1883 home encyclopedia.*

mined to be the second rank of medical prestige in Peoria. When it became popular with that group, the risk that goes with sticking one's neck out was reduced and the number-one men in the medical establishment felt free to take it up. They were followed quickly by all those who wished to appear competent and up to date. Such doctors comprised the largest group. Finally, and unfashionably late, the drug was picked up by some of those the study called Peoria's medical "eyesores"—men on the fringes, without hospital affiliations or significant practices.

Most of us, like most of Peoria's doctors, are too insecure to launch a fad ourselves. We leave that heady risk to others and, often as not, laugh as they sally out in the first zoot suit or chug off in a Model T. Should the people we most admire then swaddle themselves in zoot suits or buy Model Ts, we reconsider, and there we are—a Model T in the garage, a zoot suit in the closet, a Pet Rock on the coffee table, The Beatles on the stereo, and a hula hoop spinning in the backyard.

We can look back at most of our fads with glee, taking retrospective satisfaction in the utter outrageousness of running stark naked through the state legislature; taking a whirl in the clothes dryer; sipping hooch from a garden hose; singing "Flat Foot Floogie with a floy floy" at the top of our lusty national lungs.

And yet, satisfying as they tend to be, we never, it seems, long for the next one. Perhaps that's because, in our collective wisdom, there is the knowledge that a fad can't be wished into existence, the knowledge that somehow, somewhere, it will simply arrive.

3

*The Wizard of Menlo Park. Below, one of the faddish talking toys he licensed to keep the phonograph alive.*

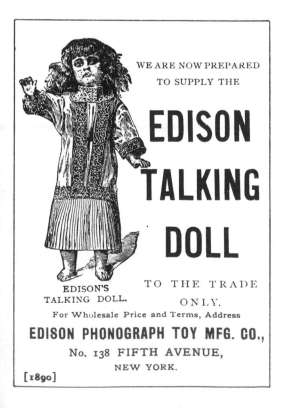

# FADS AND FAD MONGERS

From Thomas Alva Edison, left, silver-haired, benign, and nearly deaf, to the Wham-O team, opposite, purveyors of hula hoops and Frisbees— these are the American entrepreneurs who have made fads their business. None of them had it easy.

Take George Parker, who invented his first game, Banking, in 1882. No one was interested in it, so he had to take his entire life savings of $50 and a three-week leave from high school to market it himself. Henry Ford, beaming shyly from his first automobile in the photograph opposite, tried for over a dozen years to cash in on the car craze that swept the country at the turn of the century. But the snazzy motoring crowd would have nothing to do with his dismally plain design, and everybody else yelled, "Get a horse!"

Then there was Charles Darrow, an unemployed engineer suffering through the depression when he drew the first Monopoly board on a piece of oilcloth in 1933. He took it to the now-flourishing George Parker, who turned him down for no less than fifty-two reasons. A decade later, James Brunot licensed a game called Criss-Cross from his friend Alfred Butts, rechristened it Scrabble, and lost $450 his first year out. The gentlemen from Wham-O manufactured the first hula hoops in the mid-1950's, but their patent papers were faulty and they wound up facing more than forty competitors on the international hula hoop market.

Even the Wizard of Menlo Park had his problems. He made us electricity-mad with his invention of the light bulb in the 1870's and we embraced each new Edison wonder with delight—from the phonograph of 1877 to the kinetoscope of 1894, the first commercial device for viewing motion pictures. But the phonograph had to be marketed as a toy to survive, and the novelty of motion pictures had worn so thin by 1900 that financial ruin threatened. Both inventions, so it seemed, would disappear, mere faddish gadgets of a gadget-giddy era.

Eventually, success came to all the fad mongers here, bringing headaches of its own: legal squabbles, distribution foul-ups, and, as James Brunot would discover, personal and corporate taxes. "They," he sighed, "murder you."

*Henry "Get a Horse" Ford;*
*Dearborn, 1896.*

*George Parker*

*Wham-O duo Richard Knerr, left,*
*and Arthur "Spud" Melin.*

*Charles Darrow*

*James Brunot*

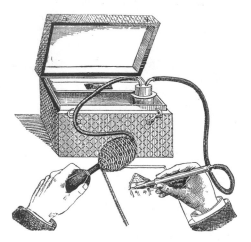

*The whatcha-ma-call-it that found a label and became a fad. Hand bellows pumped air through a container of burning benzine, turning the needle white hot.*

## THE LABEL

J. W. Fosdick didn't call it anything. A nineteenth-century artist of dubious merit, he developed a hot-iron apparatus like the one at left so he could burn classical scenes into massive wooden panels. An occasional home hobbyist discovered it and decided it was useful for decorating the odd leather box or old picture frame. And then the public found a label for it: They dubbed it "pyrography," formed pyrography clubs from coast to coast, and began burning away at pen trays, pipe racks, leather pillows, and all the bric-a-brac they could lay their hands on. Fosdick wailed that his art was being "debased," would become "merely a passing fad." And so it was: Pyrography was all the rage in 1901; by 1903 it was no more.

Most fads need labels, nicknames that make it possible for the rest of us to know what everyone else is talking about. Some labels, trade names, for instance—like Slinky and Frisbee and Silly Putty—are given at birth. Ping-Pong is a tradename, a label for table tennis that derived from the sound of vellum paddle hitting celluloid ball. That was a nickname meaningful in any language, and undoubtedly one factor behind the Ping-Pong fever that swept England, America, Mexico, and Japan in 1901.

Gibson Girl was a label, one that came long after the fact. It was 1895 by the time Charles Dana Gibson began illustrating the pages of the old *Life* magazine with his deft version of the quintessential American girl. Her hair style, her whole "look" had been faddish for some five years, but now she acquired the name that would define her. She was the Gibson Girl, and she would dominate American fashion—and the American moral landscape—for another decade. In the aftermath of World War I, she would finally disappear, done in by another girl (see left) with another name, and other morals.

*The flapper, as rendered by John Held, Jr.*

*John Kirland, above, plays professionally with a fad that came complete with label; World Frisbee Championships, Rose Bowl, 1974.*

WILLIAM JAMES HURLBUT
1901

Evelyn Nesbit, above right, was one of the American beauties who enchanted Charles Dana Gibson and inspired his Gibson Girl, above left. Evelyn's life was a scandal: She posed nude for her lover, architect Stanford White; her husband, Harry K. Thaw, shot him to death. But the Gibson Girl was above reproach. Sweetly aloof, ever cool, she was devoted to clean living—and to Ping-Pong.

Nesbit: no time for Ping-Pong.

Opposite: fad plays at fad; calendar art of 1901.

*It's 1902 and the dinner dishes have been cleared for Ping-Pong.*
*By 1903, the fad had passed.*

The "rinking" craze in New York, circa 1885. The gallery for spectators, above left, is full, and the faddists, guests at a fancy dress-and-skating ball, whoop it up on the polished floor below.

## The Audience: Outside

In 1863, the bluebloods of Newport, Rhode Island, were sighted wearing shoes with wheels. In 1975, a mashed potato pie was seen hurtling toward its target, a college dean. Suddenly, the rest of us were audience to fads.

Fads need audiences; without them, there is no one to declare the behavior faddish, and thus no fad. Most would-be faddists seek that audience—the size of the audience they attract depending on how many faddists there are and how outrageous everybody thinks their behavior is. Nine coeds at Ohio Wesleyan, below, cropped their hair in 1889 and became something of a local success, but it didn't take significantly more goldfish swallowers or pie slingers to become overnight national sensations. The number of participants couldn't have mattered less: In 1939 we stared in disbelief at the disappearance of each goldfish; in the mid-1970's we waited with bated breath for the next citizen to contact a hit man, shell out as much as $300, and choose the mashed potato pie, Boston cream, or lemon meringue that would wing its way to spouse, employer, or public official. Splat! We cheered.

The first roller skaters of 1863 may not have seemed as bizarre as pie slingers. But Dr. James L. Plimpton had designed his skates for Newport's highly visible summer residents, and so many of them laced up—virtually every ambulatory man, woman, and child in that aristocratic enclave—that the rest of us had to notice. Besides, it looked like fun. Thus, twenty years and a good cheap skate later, a local fad had blossomed into a sensational national craze.

*Twenty-four, going for twenty-five; Harvard, 1939.*

*Bull's-eye; Louisville, Kentucky, 1975.*

*Faddists nine, 1889.*

*Mary Pickford, Sweetheart of 1916.*

*The paraphernalia of Beatlemania;*
*Toronto, 1964.*

## THE AUDIENCE: INSIDE

They stepped to a dizzy ragtime beat, shocking our sense of what dancing was all about. Still, they seemed a respectable enough couple, young Vernon and Irene Castle, his spats spotless, her hats demure—and they toured, indefatigably, the big cities and out-of-the-way towns of early twentieth-century America. By 1914, the waltz was out and the Castle Walk was in. Dance records were hot, phonograph sales soared, and dancing itself—a phenomenon once confined to ballrooms and barns—was everywhere. Even restaurateurs rolled up the rugs, making room for the Gotham Gobble and the Grizzly Bear, and oh! oh! oh! that Bunny Hug!

The Castles themselves were not a fad—indeed, no person is, per se, a fad. The fad was the behavior the Castles inspired, the remarkable response on the part of their audiences that ultimately changed the nature of popular dance in America.

In the next decade, another audience would exhibit behavior that was, in its own way, equally remarkable. The marathon mania gripped us, sweeping thousands of faddists to sawdusted dance floors—and thousands more to the bleachers, faddists whose cheers and boos created, as surely as the dancers themselves, the event the rest of us called fad.

In the 1960's, rock concert audiences filled up with faddists: Kids who came in their rock- concert uniforms to smoke pot, dance, sing, strip perhaps—all as crucial to the concert as the music itself.

By then, of course, the hucksters had learned to cash in on the audience-as-faddist phenomenon. When Beatlemania struck, they were there, hustling Beatles books and buttons, posters, T-shirts, scarves, and wallets. The spinoffs raked in $50 million between 1964 and 1965—triple the receipts of American record sales in the same twelve-month period, and a hefty testament to the dollar value of audience participation.

But in the years before the Great War, there were no Irene Castle scarves, no Vernon Castle wallets. And when we fell in love with Mary Pickford a few years later, there was nothing to do but adopt her corkscrew curls, line up at the movie houses, and then wait in the dark for "Little Mary," America's sweetheart, to light up the screen.

*Above, Irene and Vernon Castle strut their stuff;*
*Eureka Springs, Arkansas, 1914.*

*Overleaf: 200,000 rock fans sing along;*
*Woodstock, New York, August 16, 1969.*

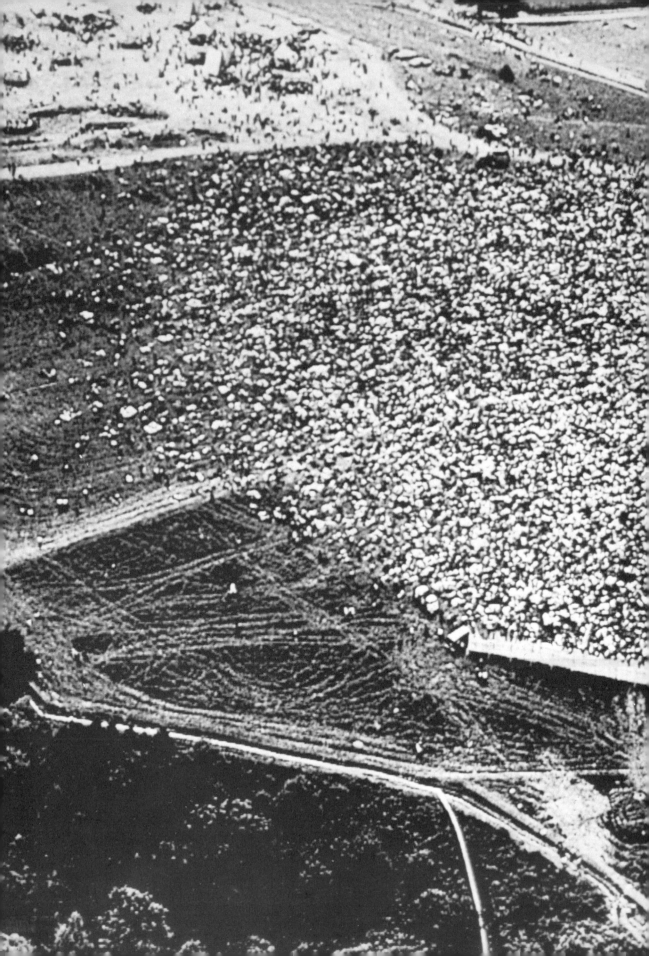

*Trickle down. From the hoi polloi of the 1860's to the middle classes of the 1880's.*

# TRICKLE UP, TRICKLE DOWN

We imported croquet from England in the early 1860's, a genteel game for the estate set to play on the rolling lawns out back. By the 1880's, croquet had trickled down to those of us in more modest circumstances, like the foursome opposite, circa 1890. Mama and Papa and a beau, perhaps, wait their turn while an apparently amateurish young lady prepares to nudge her ball across the sun-dappled green. If they are true faddists, not even fall of night will daunt their enthusiasms. Torchlit matches were big with the croquet crowd.

The game nearly disappeared after 1905, but the upper classes had abandoned it long before—as soon, in fact, as the middle classes discovered the fun. It had lost the exclusivity that was for them part and parcel of its appeal, and they rushed on to new faddish insignia of their rank. Tennis came next, golf, eventually horseless carriages—each a haven, albeit temporary, from the upwardly mobile masses of the middle classes.

As the next century wore on, the process would come to reverse itself. Fads would, with ever more persistent regularity, trickle up through levels of class, and age. But that was the remarkable exception before 1900. In the 1890's, in a rare and risqué brush with low life, society women embraced the tattoos sported by "primitives," sailors, and thieves. Jenny Jerome, Winston Churchill's mother, was among those who took the plunge, and a tattooed snake bracelet curled discreetly around her wrist forever more.

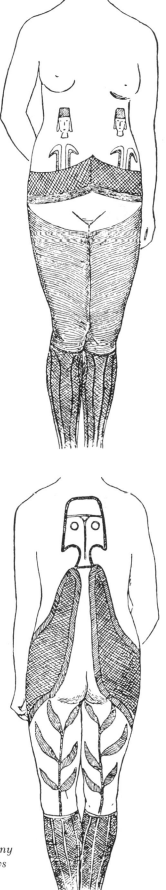

*Trickle up. From the women of Easter Island to Jenny Jerome. At right, a sketch of the front and rear views of a tattooed lady of Easter Island.*

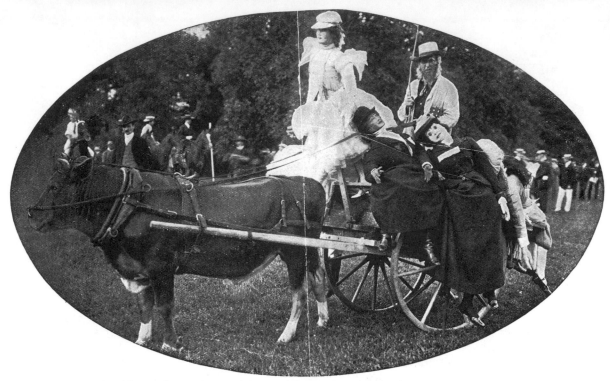

*Trickle nowhere. Above, elaborate life-size dummies crafted by the aristo-
cratic ladies of Lenox, Massachusetts, are hauled in for the races that were all
the rage in the summer of 1905—a local fad no one else bothered with. Opposite, the victors after a panty raid, an enduring college fad that trickles
neither up nor down.*

*Blue jeans: trickling everywhere, 1970's.*

*The Vanderbilt campus; Nashville, Tennessee, May, 1952.*

*A speed freak of the early 1890's, perched atop a treacherous highwheeler.*

# IT'LL NEVER LAST

America glided into the 1890's on roller skates, bumped out of the decade in a motor car—and pedaled through it all on a bicycle, caught up in a national cycling craze that lasted an impressive ten years.

Some fads burn out in ten months, or less. There was, for example, the case of the "Batman" series packaged for an adult TV audience in 1966. We were into "camp" that year, and by February the campy Caped Crusader had flapped his way to the number one spot in the nightly ratings. When ABC preempted ten minutes on March 16 so we could watch *Gemini 8* splash down to a harrowing emergency landing in the Pacific, Batman fans rose in protest. In New York alone, one thousand irate grownups phoned in to complain; three months later, they couldn't have cared less.

But the cycling craze rolled on and on: by 1896 there were between two million and four million bicycles weaving crazily around America. As late as 1899, 312 factories were still churning them out, one million strong that year alone.

Bicycles, of course, were useful, a factor that can stretch the life of any fad (cf, for instance, the CB radio); and, too, bicycles appeared before technology and the mass media bombarded us with a dizzy array of fads to choose from, the lack of competition permitting a fairly long life for a good many early fads. But first and foremost, bicycles were fast: "1 mile in 2 minutes 43 seconds," crows the highwheeler advertisement opposite. Born out of a national obsession with speed that began with the roller skate, the cycling fad sustained, and was sustained by, the larger passion that spawned it in the first place.

Some seventy years later, in a different America, a different fad would be prolonged by an equally self-perpetuating process: Born into compounds fueled by religious obsession, the children of the faddists would thrive there—and the fad would, in turn, thrive on them.

*Batman and sidekick, TV superstars of 1966.*

*A child of Krishna; Dallas, 1975.*

*"You cannot serve God and skylark on a bicycle,"*
*thundered one clergyman of the 1890's.*
*But Nanny, sedate on a low-profile model with outriggers,*
*took the twins for a spin anyway.*

## Death and Life After Life

Their parents would abandon cycling when the motorcar bumped into view, but not the teen-age misses opposite. They would pedal on into the twentieth century, ever loyal not only to the bicycle but to a good many of the fads their parents outgrew. They hung on to the roller skates of the 1880's, played Ping-Pong long after it fizzled as an adult fad in 1903—and when a jigsaw puzzle craze came and went in 1909, the kids claimed that as one of their perpetual favorites, too.

Fads that have the enduring affection of the younger generation often come back for a life after life on the larger national scene. Bicycles appear whenever we go on a national health kick; roller rinks reopened to record attendance in 1939; new Ping-Pong epidemics gripped us in the 1930's and early 1970's; and when the depression came we lost ourselves in the maze of jigsaw puzzles once more.

Very occasionally (see, for example, the overleaf) a fad doesn't die: It simply goes on and on, a permanent fixture of the cultural landscape. But that is the rarest of exceptions. For most fads, death is inevitable, and permanent. In the 1890's, we solved Pigs-in-Clover puzzles, batted a balloon around in a game called Pillow-Dex, played—avidly —a variant of checkers called Halma. Those fads are gone, not likely to pass our way again.

*Halma: gone forever.*

*Chinese nationals bring Ping-Pong back for a third rerun, 1971.*

*Jigsaw puzzles in their second incarnation, 1930's.*

George Parker having reconsidered the game he once rejected for fifty two
reasons, the Monopoly mania hit America in 1935. Twenty-two months later,
on December 19, 1936, Parker ordered a halt in production: Monopoly, it
seemed, was terminally ill. But sales suddenly rallied, and Monopoly marched
on, into the mainstream of American pastimes. Above, the Braille edition.

Monopoly is issued in fourteen foreign languages and sixteen different curren-
cies. The British have their own version (Dunhill's rosewood and leather edition, below, five thousand clams). Even the Russians, so it's said, play it,
despite an official ban.

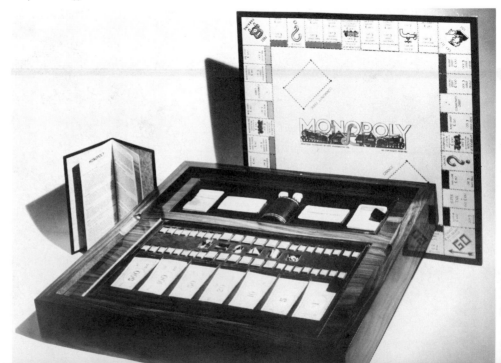

The world's second largest indoor Monopoly board; Flint, Michigan, 1972. (In 1976, the kids of Greenwich, Connecticut, did them one better with a board 98 feet square in the high school gym.)

A throw of the dice in the world's largest outdoor Monopoly game (550 feet by 470 feet); Juniata College, Huntingdon, Pa., 1967.

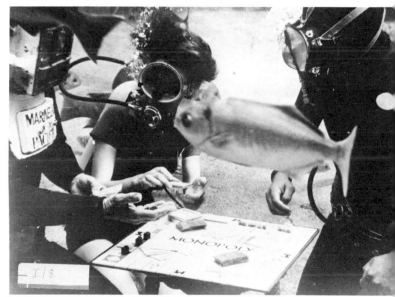

Underwater in California.

Fad, squared.

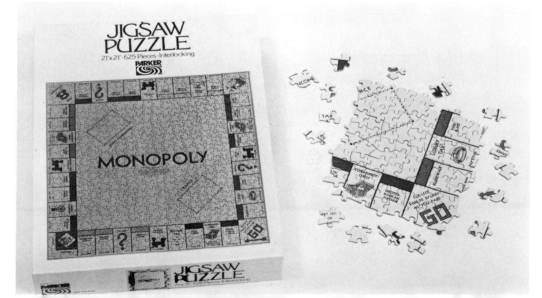

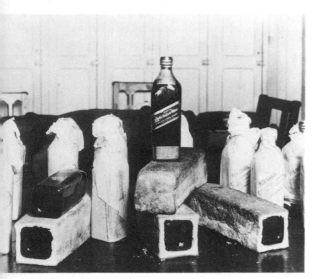

*From the bakery of the SS President Taft, 1920's.*

# FADS OF CRISIS

On April 2, 1917, the United States declared war against Germany and we hurled into a fevered state of crisis. We sang "Over There," knit socks for the boys in the trenches, prepared for the worst with "daily dozen" exercises, and, with ugly anti-German fervor, renamed familiar occupants of our landscape: hamburgers became "liberty steaks," sauerkraut became "liberty cabbage," dachshunds were "liberty pups." Likewise, when we descended into the depression during Hoover's presidency twenty years later, shanty towns like the one opposite became "Hoovervilles."

But hamburgers are liberty steaks no longer, and Hoovervilles are plain old shanty towns once again. We no longer stash our scotch in loaves of bread, one eye cocked for the G-men of the Prohibition era; no longer tend Victory gardens or burn draft cards or play The Watergate Game. Fads of national crisis, they all passed. Only the Ouija board comes back to haunt us. A domestic staple of wartime, its sales boomed during both world wars and the Korean conflict. In 1967, at the height of the Vietnam War, sales shot to an all-time high of 2.3 million, topping even Monopoly, traditional best seller of them all.

*The Ouija board, wartime wonder.*

*Hooverville; Seattle, 1933.*

*Armistice! The Great War was over at last. Drums beating, flags waving, our daily dozen exercises forgotten, we spilled into the future like champagne from a shaken bottle.*

# "Yes, We Have No Bananas"

Prohibition, ratified by the Eighteenth Amendment and enforceable under the Volstead Act, went into effect at midnight on January 16, 1920. By and large, Americans toasted the new law with a shot of gin.

Izzie and Moe, a pair of fat, jolly federal agents assigned to the Southern District of New York, would huff and puff their way through some 40,000 speakeasy raids, but the bootleg liquor kept flowing. By 1925 it would flow through 100,000 speakeasies in Manhattan alone. In Chicago, Johnny Torrio, big-time racketeer and one-time accountant, put two and two together: He and muscleman Alphonse Capone would go into the bootleg liquor business, a decision that by 1923 put Chicago in his pocket and brought Torrio an estimated personal income of $25,000 a week.

The pundits attributed it all to the war—the gin, the jazz, the mobsters, and the flappers. They blamed the new spiritualist craze on the war too, and in that they were correct: The desire to contact boys lost in the trenches had made the psychic arts faddish once again, and at the center of the craze was that bizarre talking oracle, the Ouija board.

The Ouija's stormy and oft-contested history began in the 1880's in Baltimore, Maryland, where one C. W. Kennard had an eerie—and, he decided, commercially feasible—experience with a saucer that moved around on his wife's breadboard. In 1919, some forty years and two bloody patent battles later, Kennard's

*A dig through the tombs of the ancient dead gave us one of the first crazes of the new decade. Opposite, the 900-pound solid gold mask of Tutankhamen, boy king of the fourteenth century B.C., fad hero of 1923.*

33

*The radio—even the Quaker Oats crystal set at left—gave us ringside seats at the mythic events of the era. We were with Lindbergh the misty morning of May 20, 1927, when the* Spirit of St. Louis *took off for Paris; later that year, Tunney rose from the "long count" to take Dempsey in "the fight of the century," and ten stunned members of the radio audience dropped dead of heart attacks.*

"Witch Board" had become "Ouija, the Mystifying Oracle." It was selling at the rate of one million a year, and was still figuring prominently in court cases: OUIJA CALLS HER THIEF, SO WOMAN STARTS SUIT ran one headline. And OUIJA TATTLES—$10,000 SUIT FOLLOWS.

Newspaper reporters loved it. When someone claimed that the Ouija had revealed a pair of secret weddings, that made headlines too—along with the "sugar daddies," "love nests," and "torch murders" that were filling the sensational pages of the New York *Daily News*.

They were brand new, those gory, splashy tabloid pages: The *Daily News* first hit the stands in 1919; so did *True Story* magazine. And however indiscriminate they were, mixing Ouija board mysteries with national politics, they made America—her scandals, her fashions, her newborn fads—vastly more accessible to Americans. News-hungry, we sopped it all up: newspaper circulation, 25 million as the decade began, leapt to 40 million in ten years; magazine circulation nearly tripled; and when the third member of the mass-communication triumvirate crackled to life, we embraced that too.

America's first radio broadcast came from station KDKA in Pittsburgh on election night, 1920, the announcer informing a handful of listeners that Warren G. Harding was the president-elect of the United States. Some $2 million was invested in "crystal sets" that year; by 1930 we were spending $600 million on radios. In the intervening ten years the medium gave us hundreds of jingles advertising the cars and gadgets and goods that inundated us, gave us the instant news that Leopold and Loeb had murdered Bobby Franks, gave us Fanny Brice singing right there in our very homes—free of charge. And, like the movies, radio handed us fad figures overnight.

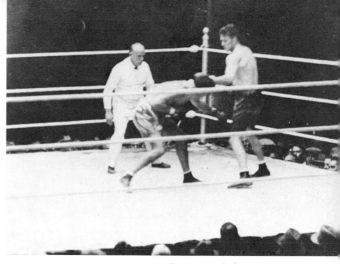

*Dempsey, left,* vs. *Tunney: a heart stopper.*

*Lucky Lindy*

Charles Lindbergh, for one, who made it across the Atlantic in a monoplane in 1927, and Gertrude Ederle, who a year earlier swam across the English Channel in 14 hours and 31 minutes, setting a new world record for the chilly paddle. Via the radio, we knew all about it instantly. By the time they came home, they were national stars—"Lucky Lindy" and Trude, nineteen-year-old wonder girl, daughter of a Manhattan delicatessen owner.

They were uncomfortable as fad figures. Quiet people, even shy, they seemed strangely out of place, implausible in an age of flagpole sitters, marathon dancers, and spit-curled starlets. But more implausible still was the first personality to dazzle us in that decade. He was Tutankhamen, an obscure Egyptian pharaoh who ruled for a brief period in the fourteenth century B.C. and died by the age of eighteen. He was Nefertiti's son-in-law, his only previous claim to fame. But when his tomb in Egypt's Valley of the Kings was opened on November 26, 1922, its incredible treasures poured forth—golden chairs and beds and jewelry, vivid frescoes and such haunting childhood relics that his life and times seemed instantly comprehensible.

The businessmen of America were typically quick on the draw, and in 1923 they flooded the marketplace with "King Tut" hats, rings, dress fabrics, and home decor. Scarab rings and bracelets were modeled after Egyptian motifs, an act of a Broadway revue was cut to make room for the new Tut number, and by the time the boy-king went back to sleep in the public imagination in the early 1930's, his name would grace babies, country estates, restaurants, apartment houses, parlor cars, and a nickel cigar.

Feeding off the international fascination with Egyptology, the King Tut craze outlasted most of the other fad phenomena that sprang up in that vintage year of 1923. That was the year of the first recorded dance marathon, the year we flocked to De Mille's original *Ten Commandments*, the year we sang "Yes, We Have No Bananas," the silly song that evolved from the confused response of a Greek fruit peddler. New York bandleader Frank Silver had asked if bananas were available, and the immigrant's answer, set to a tune from Handel's *Messiah*, sold two million copies of sheet music in 1923 alone.

Sexual rejuvenation by the implantation of monkey testicles was all the rage that year. Even if you didn't have the nerve to do it, you could read all about it in Gertrude Atherton's sensational novel *Black Oxen.* No matter that, the monkey gland operations failed; in 1923, a good many of us were convinced that wishing would make it so, that rejuvenation—or, for that matter, health, happiness, and success in every endeavor—could be ours. One simply incanted, over and over again, the self-hypnotic slogan that proclaimed, "Day by day, in every way, I'm getting better and better."

The slogan was Emile Coué's, and he had arrived in New York on January 4, 1923, his visit sponsored by Mrs. William T. Vanderbilt and the National Coué Committee. He rejected the title of "prophet" or "healer." "I have come," said the round, gentle ex-pharmacist from Nancy, France, "to help people help themselves." He proceeded to attempt just that before mass audiences along the Eastern Seaboard. In Detroit, Coué was introduced to Henry Ford. "He's got the right idea," Mr. Ford told the world. On to Chicago, where six cripples threw away their crutches, and finally Boston, where a soprano not only recovered from bronchial pneumonia with Coué's slogan but hit the high note she had longed for.

Coué went back home in February, leaving America dotted with his institutes and the AMA in an uproar. Three years later their quandary was neatly solved when the old gentleman was unable to talk himself out of a natural death. Thus Couéism faded away.

Nearly a year before Emile Coué arrived in New York with his slogans, one J. C. Babcock sailed into California bearing Mah-Jongg. He was returning from China, where he had discovered the handsome game of the Mandarins in the gambling parlors of Shanghai. Encouraged by the quick sale of the few sets he brought home, Babcock arranged for Chinese manufacture and West Coast distribution of an additional supply. The game's ancient and foreign origin, however, made for a murky copyright and patent situation, and within a matter of months a string of competitors were busy turning Mah-Jongg into the hottest national game fad of 1923.

It was a man's game in China, and there a wealthy addict might win or lose the equivalent of half a million dollars in a single evening's search for the perfect hand of fourteen tiles—four sets of three and an odd pair. Women provided the base for its success here, and while they found it too complex a game to risk heavy wagering, they were fascinated enough to buy the 130,000 sets imported in 1922, and an additional 1.5 million sets in 1923. China was running low on raw materials for the tiles by now, so Chicago meatpackers took up the slack, shipping boatload after boatload of shinbones to China—even as other traders were shipping back to America the Chinese robes, furniture, and decorative objects that had become the necessary accoutrements to the perfect Mah-Jongg party.

The fad held its own through 1923, but by 1927 the set that once sold for $25.50 was available for $1.69. According to one American driven into bankruptcy when the bottom fell out of the Mah-Jongg market, it was the crossword puzzle that ruined his business and stole our hearts.

More specifically, it was the Plaza Publishing Company's *Cross-Word Puzzle Book* that did Mah-Jongg in. Published in 1924 with Venus pencil attached, it was the first book of crossword puzzles marketed in the United States, and the trial publishing balloon of Richard Simon and M. L. Schuster. Taking as their model the puzzles that had appeared in American papers as early as 1913, they simplified and refined the form, and launched a fad so absorbing that the B & O Railroad began stocking dictionaries for its clientele. The initial trepidation of the publishers having evaporated in a cloud of cash, the Plaza Publishing Company became Simon & Schuster; by decade's end, despite competition from virtually every publisher of magazines, books, and newspapers, they sold two million copies of crossword puzzle books.

But the national penchant for filling in the blanks didn't stop at crossword puzzles. The advertising men of America's "dollar decade" had discovered the hard sell and, in an effort to refine their techniques, spent 1926 asking consumers to check their preferences in every conceivable category of goods and services. Gleefully, Americans checked away, noting their favorite toothpastes, washing machines, vacuum cleaners, toilet bowls, and canned goods.

Even the film industry latched on to the questionnaire fad, gratuitously, it would seem: certainly for the American flapper there was but one question, and but one answer. Valentino was the "bee's knees," the "cat's pajamas," their sheik. They sighed his magic name, occasionally screamed it, and when he died in 1926 of complications arising from a perforated ulcer, suicide became, briefly, a fad. One American, pictures of Valentino clutched in her hand, shot herself. Two Japanese girls flung themselves into a volcano. And in Italy, *Il Duce* himself issued an appeal begging female citizens to contain their grief.

More rational flappers made do with the sheik next door, the Joe College with the Stutz Bearcat and the patent-leather hair parted in the middle. He sported saddle shoes, golf hose, and knickers, a belted jacket and bow tie. If they were off for the weekend, his Oxford bag might contain a hot-water bottle full of "hooch"; if they were driving to a nearby roadhouse, he might carry, in addition to his ukelele or banjo, a hollow cane or some coconut shells filled with an extra supply of "giggle water"; and if the football stadium was their destination, raccoon coats would keep them warm outside while a flask form-fitted to her thigh, or a garden hose wrapped around his waist, held the secret of internal warmth.

For them, only one kind of music would do, and that was jazz. It had moved north from New Orleans on what the music industry called "race records" and in live performances by Duke Ellington, Louis Armstrong, and King Oliver's Creole Jazz Band. By 1925 Harlem had over five hundred jazz spots—including the swank Cotton Club, Connie's Inn, and the Savoy, where the college flapper crowd rubbed elbows with New York society and an occa-

sional Black, and where everybody danced that new "in" dance, the Charleston.

It did not, in fact, originate in Charleston but on the offshore islands of the South Carolina coast, where Beaufort County Blacks had danced it for years. It arrived on the mainland in 1923, to be carried north from Charleston by migrating Blacks in 1924. Harlem kids had already taken it up when Lyda Webb, star of Broadway's Black musical *Shuffle Along*, saw her ten-year-old niece Mary Scurdy "stepping it" in her home. Webb choreographed a Charleston number into her new revue, *Runnin' Wild*, and, as she said, "knocked 'em outta their seats."

Predictably though, Charleston fever didn't burn up the nation, or the world, until a white dancer, Bee Jackson, kicked it across the color line. One of the audience members unseated by *Runnin' Wild*, Jackson prevailed upon Lyda Webb to initiate her in the rites of the Charleston, and then introduced it at downtown watering spots like The Silver Slipper and Texas Guinan's El Fey Club.

A genuine issue in 1925, the Charleston was blamed for the physical collapse of Boston's Pickwick Club, a late-night tragedy that left forty-four dead. Members of the city council tried in vain to have "the dance that destroyed a building" banned in Boston. But cooler heads and the Boston underworld—which thrived on the speakeasy trade, which thrived on the Charleston—prevailed. And so did the Charleston. The Tango and the Shimmy had come before; the Black Bottom would follow in 1926. But as Bee Jackson herself said, it was the Charleston that was the emblem of the roaring, manic jazz age.

Emblematic, at least, of the gaudiest side of that gaudy decade. Kids clutched at different emblems, at Lucky Lindy and baseball cards, and at the luminaries of the burgeoning world of sports.

*Mind and body in the Roaring Twenties:*
*The 3:00 raisin break was all the rage in 1922;*
*the next year Emile Coué, right,*
*sailed into New York harbor, tipped his hat,*
*and promised to make us better and better*
*every day in every way.*

They devoured the details of Babe Ruth's life and Man o' War's, worshiped boxers Gene Tunney and Jack Dempsey, golfers Bobby Jones and Glenna Collett, tennis stars Bill Tilden and Helen Wills. They followed Johnny Weismuller through sixty-seven swimming records that spanned the decade—and then followed him into the movie houses of the 1930's when he turned his hand to swinging through the trees with Cheeta and Jane. But none of their heroes could compete with the likes of Red Grange, object of the most intense case of athlete worship in the 1920's, and of one of the first personal promotion campaigns in sports.

"Young man," said C. C. Pyle to Harold E. Grange on that fateful day in 1925, "how would you like to make a hundred thousand dollars, or maybe even a million?" The encounter between the promoter and the University of Illinois halfback took place in the lobby of C. C. Pyle's off-campus movie theater, and the proposition was attractive indeed. It was also, as it happened, an offer C. C. would make good on: Eighteen months later, a contract with the Chicago Bears—along with commercial tie-ins for Red Grange sweaters, helmets, candy bars, shoes, dolls, and sausage sandwiches—had made a millionaire out of "the Galloping Ghost" and a near millionaire out of C. C., who took 40 percent off the top.

C. C. tried tennis stars next, but he never again found a commodity quite like the kid from Philadelphia. He tried marathons, and failed. Those eerie, whimsical fad phenomena of the day, it turned out, had a life of their own, beyond the ken of even his astute eye.

Marathons began making headlines with Alvin Kelly, a one-time sailor and former boxer whose undistinguished career in the ring was characterized as a series of "shipwrecks." Thus, "Shipwreck" Kelly. In 1924 he climbed a Hollywood theater flagpole, stuck it out for 13 hours and 13 minutes (his choice—13, he said, was his favorite number), and then went home. But the word spread and soon Kelly had no lack of paying sponsors, or competitors. A Baltimore schoolgirl, for one, following in his path, occupied a backyard perch for ten days. The mayor expressed enthusiasm, and found himself presiding over a local epidemic of juvenile pole perching. No one, though, not even archrival "Hold 'em Joe" Powers, could hold a candle to the indomitable Kelly, who ate, shaved, and manicured his nails above while his manager boosted the take by selling biographical brochures below.

At the end of the decade that spawned not only flagpole

marathons but dancing, talking, kissing, eating, and drinking marathons, rocking-chair derbies, and a long-distance tango race from Santa Monica to Los Angeles, Shipwreck was employed a solid 145 days a year. In 1929, his take was $29,000.

But luck was to run out on "the luckiest fool alive." His wife left him during a forty-nine day gig in Atlantic City in 1930 ("What's the use of having a husband unless he comes home nights?" she wondered), and now the depression wiped out his backers. As late as 1942 you might have caught him perching high above Manhattan, but 1929 was, for Shipwreck, the last of the good years.

Only the marathon dancing fever seemed inexhaustible, a fad event that had trapped observer and participant alike since 1923, when the contests claimed Homer Moorehouse of North Tonawanda, New York, as their first casualty. Homer dropped dead after 87 hours of continuous dancing, but the marathons, complete with the rest breaks such incidents inspired, staggered on and on. Then, in 1928, they made the big time. That was the year Milton Crandall, Hollywood press agent, rented Madison Square Garden and announced a $5,000 prize for the winner of "the dance derby of the century."

On June 10, Crandall's three-piece band, which would alternate with a record player during the days ahead, struck up the first tune. Ninety-one couples moved onto the dance floor. Among them were some of the itinerant professionals of the trade, the "horses" like Bill Busch of Bridgeport-to-Stamford-backwards-run fame, and his partner, "Hercules Mary" Promitis, who had taken a tip from bare-knuckle prizefighters and soaked her feet in vinegar and brine for three weeks prior to the big event.

They, like most couples, survived the first days easily enough, strolling the floor, dancing a bit, chatting with the salesmen who came to peddle foot remedies, shoes, and stockings. Meals were served army-style, dished out of large vats on long tables; dance-floor hair shampoos were arranged; and cots were provided in the separate men's and women's dressing areas for the rest breaks.

Public interest picked up on the ninth day. Spectators, paying $2.20 a head, brought along gifts of clothing, jewelry, and money for their favorites. To spice up the proceedings, the master of ceremonies called for solo turns by a crowd-pleasing girl, or for an occasional "sprint" to elicit a "spray" of cash from the audience.

By the end of the second week, the competitors were getting "squirrelly." Joe Tartore had given his partner, Helen Schmidt, permission to punch him if he began to fade; Vera Campbell kicked and punched Dave Auerbach without license. Dominick Laperte delivered a shiner to partner Charlotte Cush when she warned him about leaning against the bandstand. Cush forgave Dominick on his promise to "never forget again what is due a lady," but Olive Goss was less rational. Unable to stand the sight of her partner for another moment, she beat Alois Bruhin senseless, eliminating them both from the competition. Psychological warfare was common practice, so perhaps it was a malicious, whispered suggestion that sent Mortimer Jack bolting from the floor in pursuit of an illusory pickpocket.

Twice the derby was moved temporarily to the Garden basement to make room for a scheduled boxing event. And twice came cash offers from the audience to any couple who would stop—the highest offer, $1,000, coming from Texas Guinan herself, "Queen of the Speaks." As it was, only Louis Harris, New York City commissioner of health, was able to have any effect on the proceedings: he simply closed them down in their third week. The marathon had lasted 482 hours.

For the majority who tested their endurance on those bizarre battlefields of the jazz age, the experience was brief, and a lark. For the grim competitors of the depression, however, the contests were a "tiny pocket of the human struggle," according to entertainer June Havoc, winner of one of the most grueling marathons, held in 1934 in West Palm Beach, Florida. During the last of those 3,600 hours, she kept partner "Sparky" du Pree upright by planting a pinky firmly in one of his nostrils. Their efforts earned them $40 apiece.

Writing of the days when we were willing to suffer so much for just over a penny an hour, Caroline Bird suggests that we were motivated by the vague hope that something might break for us, though by then we weren't surprised when it did not. No matter. We were engaged, she concludes, in "a ritual murdering of the enemy—time."

The 1920's did not end happily. In the aftermath of a bootleggers' war, Bugs Moran's boys, left, bloody the floor of a Chicago warehouse, victims of Al Capone's St. Valentine's Day Massacre, 1929. Later that year, Wall Street fills with mourners, opposite, as the stock market takes a plunge.

Clara Bow, the flapper with "It,"
200,000 fan letters a week,
and a King Tut ring.

F. Scott Fitzgerald,
father of them all.

The flapper as vamp.

On the beach, 1924.

## THE FLAPPER...

Clara Bow was the "It" girl and the quintessential flapper, "pretty, impudent . . . briefly clad." So said F. Scott Fitzgerald, whose 1920 best seller, *This Side of Paradise*, made him "Father of the Flapper." His fictional heroine was Roslyn— "delicious, inexpressible," he wrote of her, a "once-in-a-century blend"—and she in turn had her prototype in Zelda Sayre, Fitzgerald's bride. Zelda complained that flappers were everywhere in 1922. The Tennessee legislature agreed—and the next year banned them from public schools till they rolled those stockings back up over those knees.

*Zelda above;*
*copycat and beau below.*

*The Mah-Jongg flapper, parasol barettes clipped to her marcelled hair.*
*Assuming the lotus position, she has a go at the gambling tables in Los Angeles.*
*A Chinese god of luck, center, smiles.*

*Nazimova with Rodolpho Alfonzo Rafaelo Pierre Filibert Guglielmi di Valentina d'Antonguolla, in Camille, 1921.*

## ... AND HER SHEIK

Ex-gardener, ex-barber, ex-busboy, he was featured in the 1921 epic *The Sheik*, a film that made his fortune and finally gave the "male flapper" a name. Valentino's career as a fad phenomenon seemed destined to last forever, but on August 15, 1926, a perforated ulcer was diagnosed; on Monday of the following week, he was dead. Thus "Mad Tuesday," August 24, the drizzly day 30,000 damp fans swarmed the streets around Campbell's funeral parlor in New York, vying for a view of the body. "The rioting," said *The New York Times*, "was without precedent."

*Above, "Mad Tuesday"; below one of the few lucky fans who made it into Campbell's for a last good-bye; at left, New York City policemen surround St. Malachy's as Valentino's casket is hoisted into the Actors' Chapel.*

Gershwin, at home in Hollywood, 1931.

Satchmo, 1929.

Stepping it in the parlor
as an off-camera victrola
cranks out the beat.

## SOUND: HOT AND SWEET

It was a noisy decade. Radio sales skyrocketed, revenues of the recording business were doubling and tripling in twenty-four-month periods—and jazz, "hot" and "sweet," came roaring out of New Orleans. Louis "Satchmo" Armstrong hit Chicago and the big time in 1923; on February 12 of the following year, at a concert hall in New York, George Gershwin gave us "Rhapsody in Blue," and made the jazz fad symphonic and white. Last but not least, in 1927, Al Jolson—radiant, ageless, black-faced—belted out "Mammy" as the Warner brothers' cameras rolled on. He would launch a national fad for "Mammy" songs—and bring sound to the silent screen.

*A radio booms "Hello, folks!" in a* Life *cartoon of 1926, shattering the traditional still.*

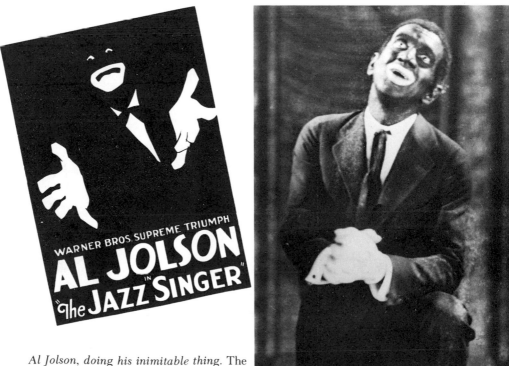

*Al Jolson, doing his inimitable thing.* The Jazz Singer, *1927.*

## BOOZE: BOOTLEGGED

It's the Ides of March, 1924, and the hard-working, cigar-chomping Fed opposite—aided by a couple of Portsmouth, New Hampshire, locals—has got himself a big one: the entire cache of a sunken rumrunner, its mast just visible at far left. An agent's life wasn't easy. A mere three miles off American shores, boatloads of booze bobbed safely up and down, awaiting stealthy emmisaries from the speaks. On shore, stashing booze away became a national rage: We hid it in hollowed-out heels of shoes, in flasks form fitted to the female thigh, in canes, perfume bottles—even beneath the folds of the raccoon coats sported by Joe College, right.

*Garden hoses full of hooch lurked beneath those hides.*

*Izzy Einstein, left, and Moe Smith, New York's inimitable federal agents. Their M.O. was disguise. "A fat man with pickles!" chortled Izzy after a successful Brooklyn bust. "Who'd ever think a fat man with pickles was an agent."*

*Texas Guinan, New York's diamond-studded "Queen of the Speaks":*
*She endured.*

*Al Capone, Chicago's big, bad bootlegger:*
*He prevailed.*

## The Mad, Mad Marathons

They swept the country in the 1920's, giving us hundreds of grass-roots celebrities. Alvin "Shipwreck" Kelly, for one, opposite and at right. He climbed to the top of his first flagpole in 1924, came down 13 hours and 13 minutes later, and spent most of the next twenty years repeating the stunt. But the 1920's were the great years for the marathons. There were eating marathons, walking marathons, running marathons, kissing marathons—and in the sun-drenched afternoons, white frocked girls and their beaux spun over the dance floor while the music played on.

*Kelly, playing the Paramount, Winter, 1930.*

*A judge makes his rounds as a Culver City, California, marathon gets underway; 1928.*

*New Yorkers launch a talkathon on Christmas Day, 1928,
the long-winded winner to claim $1,000.*

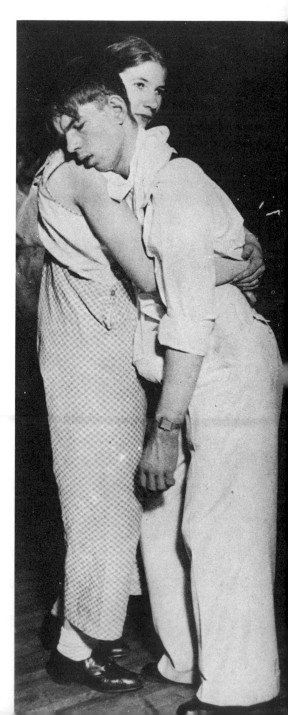

*Catnapping through the marathons, Chicago. The team above has been at it for 2,760 hours; the team at right, 3,327.*

*Milton Crandall, marathon mogul. He took the "Dance Derby of the Century" to Madison Square Garden in 1928 and made a mint.*

*"They're crazy," said Shipwreck Kelly of the dance derbyists in 1929. But Friday, October 13, 1939, found him atop the Chanin Building in Manhattan, upside down to promote National Doughnut Week.*

He was Robley D. Stevens, Drexel graduate and published author. On August 26, 1938, after bedding down for three nights in a local park, he appeared on the streets of Baltimore. "White man slave," his sign reads. "I am for sale to the highest bidder. I must have work or starve. . . . Your inquiry appreciated."

# "Brother, Can You Spare a Dime?" 1930-1945

America, said Will Rogers, was the first nation to go to the poorhouse in an automobile. It wasn't a very classy car: the 1920's ended, appropriately enough, with the bankruptcy of the Stutz Motorcar Company, manufacturer of Joe College's Bearcat.

The bottom fell out of the stock market on "Black Thursday," October 24, 1929. Only about 5 percent of the population was directly involved, but the investors made a lot of noise and controlled a lot of jobs. Within a few weeks of the Crash, the ranks of the unemployed shot from 700,000 to 3.1 million. At rock bottom, just prior to Roosevelt's inauguration in 1933, the number approached 15 million, one quarter of the labor force. Salaries had dropped by an estimated 60 percent.

The most popular ways of marking time during the depression were reading newspapers, listening to the radio, and going to the movies—in that order. A fairly narrow assortment of other temptations beckoned, but they shared one characteristic: All of them were cheap. Thus, in the spring of 1930, when the depression was worldwide, when revolutions were sweeping South America and Germans were voting for Hitler's fascism, Americans were playing miniature golf.

John Ledbetter and Drake Delanoy did not, in fact, "invent" miniature golf. The game had existed on the rolling lawns of country estates and resort hotels in the 1920's, but they were the ones who spotted a potential moneymaker in the fake-grass carpet of

*Champagne Fred on the streets of San Francisco, 1931.*

crushed cottonseed hulls patented by an El Paso entrepreneur. They laid their first course on the roof of a New York skyscraper, christened it "Tom Thumb" golf, and opened up in 1926. Business was slow, however, and so they leased southern rights to Garnet Carter of Chattanooga, who in 1929 installed hundreds of courses around Florida hotels in anticipation of the winter tourist season. Admission was fifty cents, and the Crash brought unimagined success.

The craze went nationwide in the spring of 1930, and in September, thirty thousand courses were in operation—the "Tom Thumbs," $4,500 installed, and the competing "midgets" and "Lilliputs," whose swankier spreads, priced as high as $150,000, included a swimming pool or smoking lounge. By year's end, when the fad began to wane, $125 million had been invested and the industry had taken in twice that amount. Denver was one of many towns that cashed in on the fad, instituting an annual licensing fee of $50 per course. And while one New Jersey church was

*"Happy Days Are Here Again," 1933.*

fighting unsuccessfully to protect its neighborhood from the "rowdiness" and "profanity" of late-night crowds, another installed its own course to raise money for God.

Miniature golf was cheap, novel, and co-ed—a genuine triple threat in a year when even the speakeasies were having a bad time of it. Tippling at home was cheaper, and the early depression years offered up new or rediscovered indoor pursuits to keep you there: backgammon, a British board game called Sorry—and knitting. Jigsaw puzzles were back, and for those who wanted to entertain guests but faced the problem of keeping them happy without food, there was contract bridge.

The earliest form of bridge had been created in Greece in the 1880's, auction bridge had become something of a fad when it was introduced in 1904, and an American, Harold S. Vanderbilt, had invented contract in 1925. By 1930 it was threatening to overtake whist, the most popular card game in the world at the time. The man who finally pushed it over the edge was Ely Culbertson.

An obscure and, by all reports, obnoxious Rumanian who eked out a living hustling bridge in New York clubs, Culbertson was enraged when British bridge whiz Lieut. Col. W. T. Buller made a slighting remark about American contract players. He challenged the British to a match, sailed to London with his wife, Josephine, and two younger men familiar with his system, and soundly thrashed a team handpicked by Buller.

In 1931, in the afterglow of the well-publicized challenge-match, Americans spent $10 million on bridge lessons and $100 million on all bridge products combined, including thousands of copies of Culbertson's bridge booklet and his full-length *Blue Book*. Culbertson, in 1932, alone raked in $200,000.

He wasn't the only one to ride the roller coaster from rags to riches in the depression years. But it was the awesome plunge down, taken by people like Frederick Bell, that typified the era: heir to a fortune of nearly a million dollars in 1926, "Champagne Fred" was selling apples on the San Francisco streets in 1931.

Herbert Hoover presided over the Crash, and he was universally scorned. The slums that sprang up were "Hoovervilles"; newspapers spread over park-benched bums were "Hoover blankets"; empty pockets turned inside-out were "Hoover flags"; trucks and cars pulled by mules were "Hoover wagons." And if you caught someone smiling, it was considered clever to ask if Hoover had died.

Roosevelt won the election in 1932, bringing the New Deal and a dozen "alphabet agencies." In the first five months of his administration, the Index of Industrial Production rose from 59 to 100, against the 1929 high of 125. It hardly mattered. Misery, it seemed, had come to stay, and anyone serving up a pie-in-the-sky scheme for generating income—by whatever means—could attract a mass audience of grim-faced Americans.

Huey Long, senator from Louisiana and former governor of the state, offered to make "every man a king" with his "Share the Wealth Movement." It called for a guaranteed individual income of $2,000, pensions for the elderly, and free college education for the kids. And up this sleeve, ladies and gentlemen, a $5,000 homestead for every family, a radio, washing machine, and car. The money was available, Long said—in the pockets of the rich.

He was assassinated in 1935, but for a while "the Kingfish" had been shaping up as a strong contender for president.

Howard Scott rose out of New Jersey to offer up Technocracy. Both a socio-economic explanation of the Crash and an esoteric formula for recovery, it became a *cause célèbre* in the intellectual journals of the early 1930's. In the January 1933 issue of *Harper's*, for instance, Scott explained that the Machine had made human labor obsolete, and that our price system based on the gold standard was invalid. Let our citizens work 16 hours a week, 26 weeks a year pushing the buttons of industry; base their salaries not on gold but on the ergs of energy they released in the course of production, and everyone could make the equivalent of $20,000 a year. Therein, wrote Scott, lay "the solution to the social problems of our time."

Henry Hazlitt dismissed it all as "scrambled ergs," but his pun ignored Technocracy's more sinister problems. The complexities of the erg economy would require that a select group of "technocrats" take over the government, and in anticipation of that brave day, Technocracy's ranks began to swell. Boards of governors were appointed, youth brigades were formed, and a $25 regulation gray uniform was issued—gray suit, gray shirt, gray tie, gray hat, and gray socks. The intellectuals read the handwriting on the wall, and deserted shortly thereafter.

Flashback to 1926, Royal Oak, Michigan. It's a lazy Sunday afternoon, and Father Charles Edward Coughlin is making his premier radio broadcast, a quiet interlude of homilies and inspirational messages known as "The Golden Hour," brought to you from the Shrine of the Little Flower, a wooden frame church in the Detroit suburbs. Now it's May 1935, and twenty-three thousand frenzied New Yorkers jam Madison Square Garden to hear "the radio priest" call for the nationalizing of industry and the monetizing of silver, denouncing throughout the bankers, the newspapers, the Jews, and that "great liar and betrayer," Roosevelt. The church called Coughlin "hysterical" and excommunicated him. But the leader of the Social Justice movement received more mail in 1934 than F.D.R., and national polls placed him just behind the president in popularity and power.

The most benign and most successful movement of the day came

*Francis E. Townsend, above, stumps for the dimes he plowed into publicizing his cure for the depression. One hundred million of us signed his petitions in 1935, making the Townsend movement the most popular cause in America.*

from Long Beach, California, home of Dr. Francis Edward Townsend. It began one winter morning in 1933 when, in the midst of his shaving, the good doctor glanced out his window and noticed three old women scavenging through the garbage cans for food. Townsend was shocked, and genuinely touched, and thus the Old Age Revolving Pension, OARP—known to the thousands who supported it as the Townsend Plan. Every unemployed person over sixty would receive a monthly government pension of $200. An estimated eight million to twelve million citizens would be eligible, and the plan would be financed by a 2 percent tax on business transactions of every kind. The obligation to spend the stipend in thirty days would pump the money back into the economy, production would boom, business would flourish, and all would be right with the world.

The plan was promoted by an OARP newspaper, a twenty-five-cent booklet, and the formation of Townsend clubs with ten-cent monthly dues. Within months, there were three thousand clubs in forty-two states, and by 1935, more people had petitioned Congress for enactment of the Townsend Plan than had supported any previous measure before any previous Congress in the history of the nation.

In 1936 rumors reached Washington that Townsend himself secretly considered OARP little more than a clever scheme for milking monthly dimes out of a bunch of old fogeys. Congress invited the doctor to Washington, where a four-man committee asked pointed questions about his personal finances and the income he derived from the movement. Townsend, convinced he had fallen prey to a Communist conspiracy, refused to answer further questions and was cited for contempt. A conviction and a thirty-day sentence followed.

Roosevelt was to grant him a pardon and the jail sentence would never be served, but OARP was as good as dead. Townsend faded away, muttering about the inadequacy of the Social Security Act passed the previous year.

For those who wanted to get rich quick without demagoguery, fascism, or socialism, the 1935 chain letters were a natural. The first was the Prosperity Club, and it sprang up in Denver in early April. You mailed a dime to the name at the top of a list of six, sent out five additional letters with your name at the bottom, and waited. Assuming an unbroken chain, you'd net $1,562.50 in dimes. One recipient of 2,200 letters took out an ad in the *Post* advising Denverites he wasn't about to send one thin dime to any of them, but he was something of an exception. Most people, as Denver Postmaster J. O. Stevic observed miserably, became "unhinged" at the thought of so much easy cash. His workers were assaulted with an average of 95,000 chain letters a day in the three weeks the fad lasted in Denver, many with neither address nor stamp, just a name.

It all happened so fast and so furiously that some people were bound to win: One woman reportedly received enough to bury her husband; several families resigned from the relief rolls when the dimes came rolling in; and Denver postal workers earned $20,000 in overtime during the three-week madness. It was inevitable that Stevic's department would become a cemetery for dead letters, as it did. But by that time, the craze had moved on to Springfield, Missouri.

Springfield had never seen anything like it. Chain letter "factories" were established overnight with row upon row of stenographers tapping out two letters for fifteen cents, twenty-five cents when the demand jumped. A dollar chain lured 18,000 customers in five hours, and when sidewalk promoters began hawking letters in two-, three-, and five-dollar denominations, bedlam reigned. It ended forty-eight hours after it began, leaving the people who couldn't unload their letters wandering the streets of downtown Springfield in a daze.

Federal post office officials cited lottery and fraud statutes carrying fines as high as $1,000 and up to two years in jail. With that, the burgeoning national experiments with the fad began to fizzle, leaving a persistent few to dream up chain letters supplying whiskey, kisses, or other desirables. A chain letter at the University of California offered students 26,000 dates, enough to occupy one's evenings for some seventy years.

For those willing to settle for fantasy fortunes, Monopoly appeared in 1935, a game, said *Fortune* magazine, that appeals to "the baldest acquisitional instincts." In the spring of 1935, those instincts led Americans to buy 20,000 sets of Monopoly a week. It lasted through November 1936, when sales suddenly dipped. For the moment at least, we had stopped passing "Go" and went directly to other things—among them, *Gone With the Wind*, published late in 1936. By the last months of 1937, it was selling at the furious rate of 50,000 copies a day.

Margaret Mitchell's tale of the Old South offered that most precious of commodities in hard times: escape. Earlier in the decade, thousands had followed Wang Lung through the rice paddies of China in Pearl Buck's *The Good Earth*, had taken refuge in the Shangri-La of James Hilton's *Lost Horizon*—and millions more, readers without the patience or the cash for the big, sprawling hardback novel, were devouring the short stories in the ten- and fifteen-cent "pulps." Each month, as many as twenty million of us lined up at the newsstands waiting for the Westerns and the steamy romances, for unforgettable tales of the supernatural and the action-packed adventures of hard-punching private eyes. There were over two hundred publications in all, and they gave birth, in the early 1930's, to the comic book. That format featured grown-up tales first, and was so instantly successful that within a matter of weeks, it also became a medium for the characters that the kids followed in the newspaper strips.

The most versatile of those characters—Buck Rogers and Flash Gordon, Tarzan and the Lone Ranger—darted in and out of all the mass media now—newspapers, comic books, radio, the movies—chasing hither for the kids as audience, yon for the kids as consumer. For the first time, children were creating stars, and fads. One of the first were the Big Little Books of the mid-1930's—squat, two-by-three-inch, four-hundred-page cubes that sold for a dime and offered all the back adventures of your favorite strip characters. That was only the beginning: every major character had a club, and every loyal fan was a member and thereby a purchaser of flashlights, whistles, badges, decoding rings, compasses, penknives, and charm bracelets. When Macy's announced a sale on Buck Rogers Disintegrator Ray Guns, 20,000 mothers formed a line a third of a mile long the following morning.

The Depression made for a strange assortment of culture heroes and heroines: Scarlett O'Hara, King Kong, Shirley Temple, and legions of bank robbers and parachute jumpers who won our admiration with their reckless daring. We cheered on John Dillinger and Bonnie and Clyde until they dropped, and in 1935 we assembled at local airfields on Sunday afternoons to watch "Jumping

Joe" Crane and his ilk hurl themselves off the wings of airplanes. It was a cheap show in an era that thrived on them—and radio, of course, was the greatest cheap show of all.

A third of the nation owned at least one radio, a potential audience of sixty million listeners. Every night, from 7:00 to 7:15, forty million of us tuned in to hear white vaudevillians Freeman Gosden and Charles Correll muddle through the complications ensnaring "Amos 'n Andy" and the Black lodge members of the Knights of the Mystic Sea. President Roosevelt listened along, and during the broadcasts, telephone use across the nation dropped 50 percent.

"Our Gal Sunday" and some of the very soaps we know and love today filled seven solid hours of air time by the end of the decade; crime shows like "Gangbusters" took off from the shoot-'em-up headlines of the era; "The Goodwill Hour" offered miniscule prizes to studio-audience members who would share their personal tragedies with the folks at home—and made the question, "And what is *your* problem, Madam," a faddish national joke.

Joe Penner's question seemed even funnier. As a second-string comedian on a southern vaudeville tour in 1931, he had sailed out of the wings one night to rescue an inept MC who was dying fast. "Wanna buy a duck?" was the line that came off the top of his head. For reasons that may forever remain obscure, it seemed positively inspired to 1930's audiences. Penner went on to guest appearances on Rudy Vallee's show, and to his own show a few weeks later. Radio comics like Jack Benny and Fred Allen would stick with us through two more decades; Penner didn't. But it's been estimated that the forgotten comic, who himself recognized that it wouldn't last, made a quarter of a million dollars from each of those four lucky words.

Dozens of comedians cashed in on radio—and dozens of musicians: Phil Spitalny and his All-Girl Orchestra, featuring Evelyn and her Magic Violin; Joe Spivak and his Serenaders, coming to us "direct from the beautiful Bamboo Room in the Hotel Belton in the heart of downtown Des Moines," where they asked the musical question, "Brother, Can You Spare a Dime?" Radio made Vallee and Crosby stars, and was the financial mainstay of the "big bands" of Benny Goodman, Artie Shaw, the Dorsey Brothers, Glenn Miller, Harry James.

Each band recorded classics with which it became identified, but the particular song hardly mattered. It was the band's sound that mattered, and the sound had to be "swing." "It don't mean a thing," ran a line from a Duke Ellington hit of 1932, "if it ain't got that swing." It was music for dancing, and the dance, in all its dazzling variations, was the Jitterbug. There was the Big Apple and the Boogie-Woogie, the Shag, the Susie-Q, the Lindy Hop, named for Lindbergh's flight, and the hip-wiggling, finger-wagging strut called "Truckin'." It was all Jitterbugging, and it was big business. In 1936 Victor alone issued nine hundred thousand dance records, most of them swing music for the Jitterbuggers.

Like the flappers and sheiks before them, Jitterbuggers had their emblematic costumes, the 1930's bringing an early form of unisex fashions: boys and girls both wore baggy sweaters and saddle shoes, and later, shirttails, jeans, and bobby sox. Borrowing their slang from the argot of Black musicians, they would troop downtown to dance in the aisles while Goodman "greased that licorice stick," Krupa "beat his skins," or James "blew his plumbin'." It knocked the kids out, and back home they'd spin a couple of discs for the other hepcats, and cut that rug.

By decade's end, Jitterbuggers of the high school set were playing charades and telling the terrible "knock-knock" jokes that yielded to "Confucius say" in 1940. "Confucius say chemist who fall in acid absorbed in work." This and other equally hysterical one-liners were printed on dress fabrics and appeared in national magazine ads, newspaper contests, and popular songs.

College fads hit an all-time preposterous high in April 1939 with the sudden outbreak of goldfish swallowing. The mania began when Harvard freshman Lothrop Withington, Jr., displaying his aquarium to a classmate, casually mentioned that he had once eaten a goldfish. A $10 wager induced a repeat performance. and within weeks college men and an occasional woman had taken to public swallows of, in addition to goldfish, angleworms, beetles, phonograph records, gunpowder, and live white mice. Salt, pepper, and ketchup were seasoning; milk, orange juice, and soda were the chasers. Despite legal threats by animal preservation societies, doctors' warnings of tapeworm infestation, and the formation of student Societies for the Prevention of Goldfish Eat-

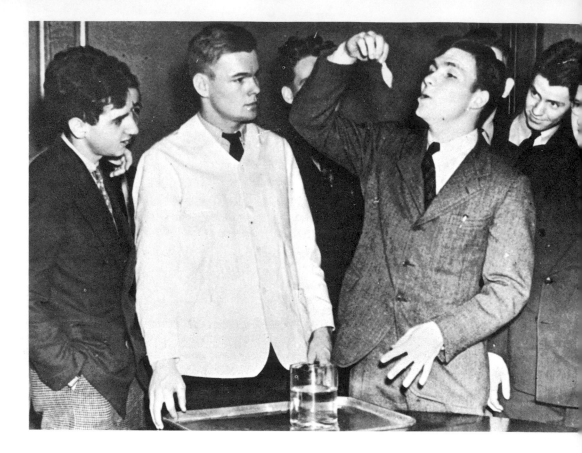

ing, the exhibitionists swallowed away, the record of 210 fish going to a St. Mary's University sophomore.

For the more conservative citizen of 1939, the roller rink was the platform for a considerably less outrageous exhibition. Roller-skate dancing was in, bringing as many as 7,000 faddists a week to each of the nation's 3,500 refurbished roller rinks. Waltzes, Tangos, and Fox Trots wafted from the (gee, Dad, it's a) Wurlitzer, along with the tunes for new rink dances like the Chicken Scratch, the American Promenade, and the Howdy-do. At the height of the renaissance, the "skatarina" appeared, the dress whose circular skirt and matching bloomers saved us from increasing exposure to female panties.

At the local movie houses, the National League of Decency tried to see to it that titillating influences weren't available on the silver screen either. Long kisses, double beds, and nude babies were forbidden. But Mae West thrived anyway, along with Garbo, Har-

*Lothrop Withington, Jr., opposite, downs that first fateful goldfish; Harvard, March 3, 1939.*

*John Patrick developed a taste for music, the menu including "Deep Purple" and "Who's Sorry Now?"; University of Chicago, 1939.*

low, Joan Crawford, and smoky-eyed Clark Gable, who "frankly, my dear," didn't give a damn.

But when our pockets were empty, there was still an easy chair and the radio. To the gentle strains of "It's a Lonesome Old Town When You're Not Around," band leader Ben Bernie wound down the evening. "And so it's time to say good night. . . . Yowsah, yowsah, yowsah. This is the old maestro and all the lads bidding you a fond cheerio, a bit of pip, pip, pip, toodle-oo, au revoir, and pleaassant dreeaams."

On December 7, 1941, it was the radio too that brought the news to millions of Americans that their lives were about to change, utterly. A Japanese strike force had bombed Pearl Harbor, so we put our whimsies in a back pocket, and we went to war.

The few fads that appeared in the war years were low key and war-oriented. A foot soldier, for example (or so one story goes), could no longer contain his irritation at the Air Force boast that it

# Your Ads can help Shorten the War by supporting the WOMANPOWER campaign

### The More Women at War—
### The Sooner We'll Win

Women by the millions must work in war plants— carry on vital civilian services—release men for combat by joining the WAVES, WACS, SPARS and MARINES—because even though shifts in schedules occasionally cause local, temporary layoffs—*the manpower situation grows tighter every day.*

Millions of women are already in war work. But millions more must be recruited—*mostly from among*

*women who do not yet realize how badly they are needed.*

This is a tremendous educational job. The women of America must be made to realize that in wartime, just as men of military age must *fight*, women of working age must *work*. This requires repetition of facts and appeals which only advertising can provide.

Many national advertisers have already helped— many are continuing to help—but much more advertising support is needed.

For official, government-approved information concerning the "overall" womanpower campaign, write to War Advertising Council.

## Your Advertising can help fill these War Jobs!

**WAR PLANTS**
Production cannot meet demands of the armed services unless women who have never worked before take jobs in war factories.

**CIVILIAN SERVICES**
Women are needed to step into the shoes of men leaving vital civilian jobs for services in the armed forces.

**ARMED FORCES**
Hundreds of thousands of women must be recruited as replacements for soldiers, sailors and marines needed for combat duty.

---

**Some Other
War Campaigns Needing
Advertising Support**

Absenteeism

Anti-inflation

Cadet Nurse Recruiting

Conservation of Critical Resources

Food Fights for Freedom

Information Security

V-Mail

---

## WAR ADVERTISING COUNCIL, INC.

**60 East 42nd Street, New York 17, New York**

*A non-profit organization representing all phases of advertising, created to mobilize the power of advertising for Victory.*

was always "first on the spot." He scrawled "Kilroy was here" on a wall and thus launched the most memorable fad of the era, for "Kilroy," in all his thousands of manifestations, now turned up at most stateside bus stations, at the torch held aloft by the Statue of Liberty, and in the john reserved for the Allied leaders at Potsdam.

High-school boys wore combat boots during the war; girls wore combat boots—plus, affecting a superficial maturity, lipstick, eye makeup, and rouge. The term "teen-ager" was coined during wartime, dignifying the adolescents who had become invaluable in the scarce labor market. Even the younger teen-age girls found lucrative enterprise, baby-sitting for the mothers who worked the night shifts at munition plants. On their off nights, girls went to faddish slumber parties. Decked out in pj's and nighties, they wrote letters to boyfriends overseas, knit the argyle socks that went into "Bundles for Britain," and listened, feverishly, to the impeccably crafted sound of Frank Sinatra, "The Voice."

Manufacturers of records, phonographs, and jukeboxes were among the first to take advantage of the new, moneyed teen-age market. In 1940, half a million jukeboxes took in half a billion dollars; in 1946, twice as many boxes would swallow three times as much small change; 775 record companies sold over 300 million records that year.

Country music was popular during the war, slicker and more polished than the hillbilly sound faddish in 1935. Jazz took up a large share of the rest of the market—big band jazz, the "bop" jazz of Charlie Parker, and the "cool" jazz of Thelonius Monk. But all of them, even "The Voice," had stiff competition from "Rosie the Riveter." Fictional subject of a hit song, Rosie glorified the members of the "womanpower" campaign and became a poignant symbol to a country immersed in gas and food rationing, victory gardening, and national drives for scrap metal and paper, for the bacon grease that went into explosives, for the nylon stockings that went into gunpowder bags and parachutes. Rosie, pop heroine, sold a solid 3.5 million records in 1944 alone.

Six months later, the war was all but over. Victory in Europe came in May 1945; in August, Harry Truman called the hardest shot and dropped the bomb. Hiroshima and Nagasaki ended the war, and the war ended the Depression. Perhaps nothing else could have.

*The Womanpower campaign cranks up, fueled by the War Advertising Council, Inc. Its members mobilized "the powers of advertising for Victory." The rest of us tended Victory gardens, bought Victory bonds, licked Victory stamps, and sent them through the V mail. We won.*

June 1931

# The Illustrated
# DETECTIVE MAGAZINE

10¢ IN U.S.
15¢ IN CANADA

*Thrilling Fic...* *...teries of Real Life*

The Most
UNUSUAL
MYSTERY
MAGAZINE
You Can Buy
At Any Price

The
SINISTER
SECRET
of the
SCARLET
ROOM—

JOHN
RUSSELL
Tells the
Inside Story
of the
Elsie Sigel
Case!

# COUNTERFEIT!
## The New Complete Thriller
### *by*
# EDGAR WALLACE

# THE MYSTERY OF BEAUTIFUL MARY ROGERS
# THAT DEFIED JUSTICE FOR 100 YEARS
# Is It Now Solved by Val O'Farrell?

*The pulps—peaking at ten million readers a month by mid-decade.*

## HARD TIMES, CHEAP THRILLS

"It wasn't a fun night," said one Algonquin Round Table wit of the evening of October 29, 1929. "I mean, that afternoon, everybody had lost every shirt he had."

So the depression came; beyond lay the war. Through it all, we sought escape—cheap. On these and the following pages, a portfolio of the crazes, fevers, and fancies that got us through Hard Times.

*At right, the first zoot suit on record, photographed in the early 1930's. The hepcats of Harlem were first to swath themselves in its cozy folds. By the 1940's, it was all the rage. "Three to six inches of padding at the shoulders," moaned Newsweek, "dripping soggily almost to the knees."*

*Wallis Simpson beelines for the limo waiting on a London street, 1936. For Edward VIII, she was "the woman I love"; for the rest of us in the glamour-starved thirties, she was an ever-faddish figure of a fairytale romance.*

# STARTING SATURDAY

*It was the age of "talkies" and "the little tramp" still didn't utter a word. No matter. He masqueraded as a rich man in City Lights, and in October 1931, the lines began forming at dawn.*

**HIS MOST ENTHUSIASTICALLY AWAITED COMEDY ROMANCE IN PANTOMIME**

*Charlie*
## CHAPLIN
*in* CITY LIGHTS

## DIME-A-DAY CHAIN LETTERS STILL FLOOD MAILS DESPITE GOVERNMENT WARNING

## POSTAL FORCE LABORS LATE INTO NIGHT SORTING 165,000 DENVER CHAIN LETTERS

*Denver gave birth to the chain-letter craze; Springfield, Missouri, was next. Above, Denver Post headlines for April 20 and 28, 1935.*

*Dillinger, John Herbert; pop hero. He lived our fantasies: He stole from the rich and kept it. Opposite, the portrait that appeared on the wanted poster J. Edgar Hoover issued, June 25, 1934.*

*A sober crowd gathers at a Chicago street corner the evening of July 22, 1934. Moments before, his girl on his arm, Dillinger had strolled out of a movie house and down the block. G-men lying in wait plugged him on the spot. The film was Manhattan Melo-drama; the star was Clark Gable; the wounds (see bloodstains above center) were fatal.*

*Dillinger's straw hat, wire frames, and that last cigar.*

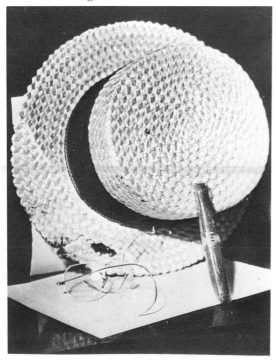

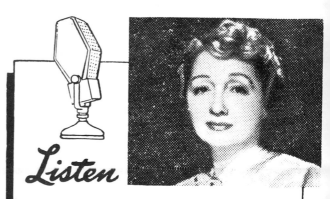

## Listen

# TO HEDDA HOPPER'S "Hollywood Discoveries"

**A** brand new type of radio show—featuring your star-reporter—Hedda Hopper. Discover how stars are born, how "breaks"—which might come to any of us—skyrocket unknowns overnight. It's the real inside story of Hollywood as revealed by one of movie-land's most charming stars, often referred to as "Hollywood's best dressed woman." The laughs, loves, oddities of the movie people—by one of them.

**Acclaimed as Hollywood's greatest "inside story"**

# XWZ TUES. & THURS. 10 A·M

*"Listen!" the ad at right exhorted us.*
*We did, two nights a week,*
*dreaming of stars and lucky breaks.*

*The Paramount, New York, October 12, 1944. "The Voice" is onstage—live. Outside, the ticket office caved in under the weight of 10,000 more bobbysoxers stampeding for seats.*

*"The Voice," on the air for NBC.*

*Sinatra had his skeptics (center and far right at the Hollywood Bowl, 1943). But all of us tuned into the team below right.*

*Amos, a.k.a. Freeman Gosden.*

*Andy, a.k.a. Charles Correll.*

*Below, Gosden and Correll on the air for CBS.*

# COME TAKE A JOY RIDE THROUGH THE SKY!

See this grand, breath-catching climax of all screen musical entertainments! . . . A picture that gaily spurns the earth and chases Folly among the stars!

DOLORES DEL RIO

# "FLYING DOWN TO RIO"

Heart-racing romance . . . so daring, so different . . . that your wildest dreams of a "music show" will come to enchanting fulfillment! . . . Thrilling stars, teasing tunes, delirious fun and gorgeous girls in scenes of ravishing beauty . . . The year's most exciting revel in the theatre bids you "Happy landing"!

with

## DOLORES DEL RIO

GENE RAYMOND · RAUL ROULIEN
GINGER ROGERS · FRED ASTAIRE

Music by VINCENT YOUMANS
An RKO Radio Picture directed by Thornton Freeland
MERIAN C. COOPER, Executive Producer
Louis Brock, Associate Producer

Hear these tantalizing songs: . . . "Music Makes Me" . . . "Orchids in the Moonlight" . . . and the new dance sensation that will soon be sweeping America . . . the hypnotising, compromising "Carioka"!

GENE RAYMOND

RAUL ROULIEN

FRED ASTAIRE    GINGER ROGERS

*Music and magic on M.G.M.'s big silver screen, 1931.*

*Fad west: Mount Baker, Oregon; September, 1930.*

Mini worlds were big in the 1930's. Tom Thumb Golf made Garnet Carter, below, a millionaire by 1931. In 1935, Marvin Gardens was yours for $260. Sold!

Carter, putter.

*Fad east: Florida, Spring, 1930.*

*Scarlett O'Hara knelt in the dust and ashes of the Civil War and swore she'd never go hungry again. We bought it—at the rate of 50,000 copies a day. Above, her author, Margaret Mitchell—wide-eyed with the Pulitzer Prize and the flood of congratulatory cables that followed, Atlanta, May 1937.*

*More heroines: Clara, Lu, and Em were the faddish, folksy stars of
radio's first daytime serial. On the air and off (above, an ad from
Ladies'* Home Journal, *June 1932), they pushed the product that gave
the soap opera its name.*

*Superstar Josephine Baker in sequined splendor.
She took le jazz hot to Paris, then Berlin,
and at right, bounces back to Broadway,
bearing the Conga, February 1936.*

*The Conga takes off. Above, popular demand brings twenty of Arthur Murray's best aboard the S.S. Illinois, December 1940. Opposite, it's the Conga plus the Lindy Hop plus an Australian import called the Kangaroo Jump. They dubbed it all the Harlem-Conga and unleashed it at the Savoy, January 1941.*

*Harry James blows his plumbin'.*

*Tommy Dorsey, swingin' sweet.*

*Big-band-beat feet.*

*The feet go on, Central Park, 1946.*

*New Jersey, 1939.*

*Truckin' up Broadway, 1935.*

*Above, the Tivoli Dance Hall, Copenhagen;
below, Madison Square Garden.*

*The zoot suit fad flourished in the early war years. Even pilots, above, adapted it, pumping it up to maintain normal flow of blood to the brain at high speeds. Meanwhile, down on the street, the zoot suit was in big trouble.*

*Los Angeles, June 7, 1943. Servicemen, above, mob a streetcar in search of zoot-suited hoodlums. They found them: below, the zoot suiters, minus zoot suits. Los Angeles, and eventually the nation, banned zoot suits for the duration.*

*The zoot suit war and then the Big War were over. Tokyo Rose, above, fad phenomenon of the Pacific front, was behind bars, and we barreled into the boom years.*

# "It's Howdy Doody Time!" 1946-1959

In a classic comedy routine from the late 1950's, Mel Brooks as the "2000-Year-Old-Man" is asked what the means of transportation was in the days of "rocks and caves." "Mostly fear," he replies. "An animal would growl, you'd go two miles in a minute." So it was in America after World War II. Fear transported us, and the growl was Russian.

The war ended in the summer of 1945, and the following spring, Winston Churchill spoke of the "iron curtain" that had descended across Europe. The Cold War, so labeled by financier Bernard Baruch in 1947, was on. Through the following years, whether painting-by-number or watching "Dragnet," eating frozen food or brushing our teeth with chlorophyll, we were a paranoid lot, one eye cast over our national shoulder, waiting for the sneak attack.

In fact, the attack seemed imminent. The Russians had grabbed Berlin and in 1949 they successfully tested their own A-bomb. China had fallen to the Communists; South Korea teetered on the brink. The Red Menace surrounded us—had infiltrated us: the House Un-American Activities Committee started its investigation in 1947, and within the year a good many of us were convinced that Communists lurked under every bush. When the obscure junior senator from Wisconsin, Joseph P. McCarthy, took up the cry in 1950, the Great Fear was already at fever pitch. An electrical

*Fads of the postwar boom years lived, and died, on the TV sets newly installed in our living rooms. The Army-McCarthy hearings of 1954 gave us a long, hard look at Joseph McCarthy, opposite; on the thirty-sixth day of televised battle, we decided we'd had enough. Howdy Doody and Buffalo Bob, above, endured—a daytime kiddy-hour fad that packed the peanut gallery from 1947 to 1960.*

short circuit brought a New York subway to a halt one day that year, somebody shrieked "The Russians!" and a thousand people stampeded in panic.

The unnerving gongs of the air raid drill echoed through our elementary schools monthly. With quiet excitement, the little troopers scrambled under their little desks, chins tucked, arms clasped behind their heads, eyes and ears covered. Those Commies weren't going to catch *them* napping.

Concrete and steel fallout shelters began to appear in 1950; prefab models followed, complete with wall-to-wall carpeting. As the decade progressed, bomb shelters suggested a new form of endurance contest, with individuals and couples competing to see who could stay cooped up the longest. The record was set in 1959 by a newlywed Miami couple who spent their two-week honeymoon twelve feet under—playing gin rummy, they said.

A year earlier, "fast gun" clubs had appeared to give super-patriots a chance to prepare for a more conventional, face-to-face confrontation. Offering drawing and shooting practice with wax bullets fired at a wooden silhouette, the fast-gun clubs attracted truck drivers, factory workers, firemen, cops, and an occasional student—anyone, said a club president, "with a secret urge to pit himself against the badman." Timers attached to the guns registered record drawing speeds of $\frac{13}{100}$th of a second, a good $\frac{20}{100}$th faster than those credited to the gunslingers of the Old West. Jesse

*St. Petersburg, Florida, 1952.*

*Everywhere, USA.*

James wouldn't get far here, and neither would Khrushchev's attack force.

With our eyes on the horizon searching for those nefarious Russian bombers, we still had hands, feet, and a mouth to be occupied elsewhere. One of the first things to melt in that mouth after the end of World War II sugar rationing was ice cream: in 1946, a record 714 million gallons slid down the national gullet, much of it in slurpy sodas, sundaes, and banana splits. A few years later we discovered the great fad food of the next decade.

In 1949, pizza was confined to America's Italian colonies, and the *Atlantic Monthly* brought the good news to the rest of us: "You eat it, usually, sitting in a booth in a bare, plain restaurant, with a mural of Vesuvio on the walls, a jukebox, and a crowded bar. The customers are Italian families, Bohemians, lovers, and—if a college is nearby—students and faculty members." By 1955, pizza eating was a fad—*the* thing to do after the school sock hop—and pizza threatened to replace the avuncular hamburger as the teens' favorite snack.

*Fear fads of the 1950's had us searching the skies for UFOs, Russian bombers, and clouds of radioactive dust. We brewed vats of conciliatory coffee for the saucermen, trained kids to "duck and cover"—and by 1960, even Kokomo, Indiana, had a fallout shelter, opposite, crammed full of Campbell's soup, Frosted Flakes, and Reynolds Wrap.*

*One lone farmhouse, lower left, holds out against Levittown, Pennsylvania. All of us managed to hold out against the Edsel, opposite.*

Our extraordinary ingestion of ice cream and pizza was not an isolated phenomenon. After twelve years of the Great Depression and three and a half of world war, the United States was barreling into the boom years. Bigness, immoderation, "conspicuous consumption"—all condemned, even outlawed, during wartime—were everywhere: in food consumption, child-bearing, housing, dress, transportation, entertainment. Advertising revenues skyrocketed, rising faster than the GNP or any other business barometer. Teen-agers had joined the list of consumer target groups during the war, and television would make consumer trainees of toddlers born during the postwar baby boom.

Increasingly over the years, those babies were born in suburbia, the postwar answer to the urban housing squeeze. Sprawling ranch houses were voguish among the well-heeled in 1946, and for the bargain hunters William Levitt arose in 1949, converting Long Island potato field into prefabricated suburbia. For $60 a month and no money down, $7,990 bought you four rooms and an attic, a washing machine, outdoor barbecue, and a 12½-inch TV set built into the living room wall. The houses were as alike as the potatoes had been, but when Levittown was completed in 1951, its 17,447 units were home to 82,000 people and had already become the prototype for the carbon copy community.

Predictably, suburban spread led to fads in home decorating and design. Interior white woodwork was in and out by 1950, and the living room now featured three walls painted one color, the fourth in another color or covered with wallpaper. Picture windows were a fad. Millions of us stuck one in somewhere, even if it framed the neighbors' garbage cans or our own detached garage.

Those garages were, of course, filled with the cars that had made suburbia possible in the first place. There were 23 million privately owned automobiles in 1929, only three million more in 1945. But in the postwar car-and-suburb symbiosis, the number more than doubled. In 1955, our expanding interstate highway

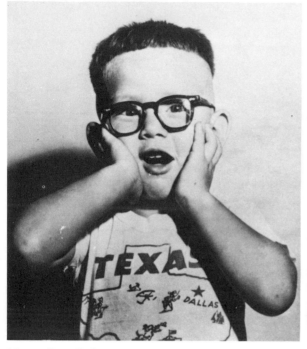
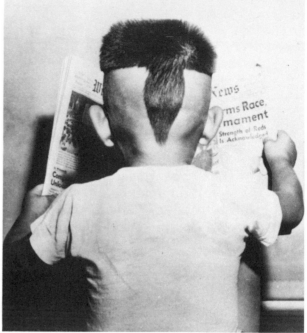

*Master Powell, front.*　　　　　*Master Powell, rear.*

system was host to 54 million newer, bigger, flashier cars—which got bigger and flashier as the "bigger-is-better" decade rolled on, reaching their most outlandish proportions with the tailfin fad of 1957 and 1958.

The fashion industry took advantage of the end of wartime shortages, stocking the ready-to-wear racks with the voluptuous goods inspired by Dior's "New Look." Natural shoulders, padded bustlines, and nipped-in waists descended to full-flowing skirts that ended a foot from the floor. The demand for high heels and ankle straps soared as women jumped at anything to emphasize that mere twelve inches of exposed leg. Dior's silhouette dominated women's fashions until 1957, when Europe gave us the "sack" and the "bag." Those monstrosities died fast, but the tide had turned: the "New Look" had become the old look.

The Dior decade put girls in full skirts too. In 1951 those skirts ballooned above a sea of crinolines, and the stylish teen was wearing a poodle-cut above, saddle shoes below, and if she lived to be so lucky, her steady's varsity sweater. In 1954, the poodle-cut was out, but felt skirts with appliqued poodles were very in. Two years later, long hair was back, with a decided preference for the

*Heroes of the Fabulous Fifties. Davy Crockett was "King of the Wild Frontier," killed him a b'ar when he was only three. Robert Eugene Powell, a toddler from Texas, settled for a coonskin haircut. Tab Hunter, blue-eyed, blond-haired, was all the rage. The eyes presented a problem, but the hair came straight out of a bottle, right.*

*The Tab Hunter brew.*

ponytail. A-line skirts were big, and steadies were exchanging dog tags with each other's names.

The boys, still a long way from ponytails themselves, were sporting crew cuts and flat tops ("fabulous!"). These were often topped by an Ivy League cap with a buckle in back—"tremendous!" Blazers were everywhere, and dirty white bucks: only a nebbish would wear clean ones. And if you weren't a weenie or a yo-yo, your pants had a buckle in back too. So, for that matter, did your Bermuda shorts, and your girl's Bermuda shorts, and your dad's Bermuda shorts—unless he was some kinda banana.

There were, of course, departures from the teen-age uniforms. Some sophisticated circle-pinned girls might step out in the All-American straight skirt and matching pastel sweater favored by the college set. And one subculture of teen-age boys departed from custom all the time: "greasers," "skids," "rocks," whatever the regional argot, they wore ducktail haircuts and black leather jackets, their T-shirt sleeves rolled over a pack of smokes and bulging biceps.

Men's campus fashions offered two possibilities: the button-down Ivy League look, or the pegged pants, padded-shoulder

*James Dean, a hero for the 1960's.*

jacket, and open-necked Hawaiian shirt that branded students in the Middle West. In the business world the "Madison Avenue look" prevailed. The "man in the gray flannel suit" (charcoal) wore a button-down shirt (pink), bow tie (skinny), and a narrow-brimmed hat (olive).

Even the "consumer trainees" had their fashion fads—30 million kids, for example, wore propeller-topped beanies in 1952. But it was cowboy duds that dominated. Hopalong Cassidy had appeared on the home screen in 1948, and $40 million of Cassidy clothing were riding the range by 1950. As the decade progressed, Hoppy was joined by Gene Autry, Roy Rogers and Dale Evans, and the Cisco Kid—all absolute inspirations to the young cowpokes, who herded up $283 million in toy guns, spurs, boots, chaps, and lassoes between 1955 and 1959.

Once they had recognized the extraordinary potential in the kiddy market, fad mongers flooded it with a vast assortment of

106

*Heroes of the Fictional Fifties. James Dean, opposite, was the star of Warner Bros.' 1955 super-release,* Rebel Without a Cause. *A decade later, the character he created—brooding, agonized, and alienated—played on in our memories of the way it was. In the 1970's, ABC's "Happy Days" gave the fifties to the Fonz, a finger-snapping, gum-chewing greaser with a heart of gold. He revised our memories again, and made Henry Winkler the biggest fad superstar in history.*

*Winkler, a Fonz for the 1970's.*

goods. The kids bought Slinkys, which walked downstairs; and rediscovered baseball cards, the turn-of-the-century cigarette premium that now came as a bonus with bubble gum—or vice versa, depending on your priorities. Between 1949 and 1954, they bought 32 million little blobs of the silicone residue called Silly Putty, and the following year, when "the King of the Wild Frontier" rode out of the woods, the kids bought him too, and set the marketplace on its ear.

According to the Walt Disney legend, Davy Crockett was "born on a mountaintop in Tennessee." According to Davy's debunkers, that was about all the legend shared with reality. "The historic truth," said John Fischer, editor of *Harper's*, "is that Davy Crockett was a juvenile delinquent who ran away from home at the age of thirteen. . . . When he claimed that he had shot 105 bear in nine months, his fellow tipplers refused to believe a word of it on the sensible ground that Davy couldn't count that high."

But from May to December 1955, truth was hogwash and coonskin was pure gold. During the seven-month boom, an estimated four million records and 14 million books were sold to a new generation of little pioneers. The demand for Crockett caps sent furriers scurrying after used raccoon coats and boosted the wholesale price of raccoon tails from twenty-five cents to as high as $8 a pound. Dime stores devoted up to seventy feet of counterspace to some three thousand items—powder horns and rifles, bath towels and telephones, ukeleles, lunch boxes, and ladies panties. By Christmas, Davy T-shirts had been reduced from $1.29 to thirty-nine cents, and still weren't moving. While it lasted though, $100 million had changed hands in the name of the embattled backwoodsman. Not surprisingly, Mrs. Margie Flowers Cohn of Okawville, Illinois, officially certified as Crockett's closest living descendant, didn't see a nickel of it.

In 1957, two years after Crockett was old hat, three young New Yorkers discovered a dirt-cheap supply of old raccoon coats stockpiled by a furrier who couldn't unload them when the Davy craze fizzled. Stan and Sue Salzman and Ben Bejan presented them to their guests at a Christmas party, word got around to the campuses, and a mini-raccoon renaissance was on. It lasted while the supply did, but that wasn't very long.

Over the next six months, the trio salvaged another 400 coats from used-fur dealers and were getting bored with the whole business by June when *Glamour* ran a photo of one of their coats and listed them as suppliers. Lord & Taylor ordered 200 that sold in the store's College Shop for $25 apiece to customers who began gathering at dawn. Gimbel's and S. Klein's got into the act, and a handful of lucky collegians unearthed free raccoons in their parents' attics. Lord & Taylor sweet-talked the Salzman group into tracking down 1,200 more, but a few weeks later the well ran dry. Before the Davy Crockett fever, an estimated 2 million raccoon coats were unemployed in America. The two or three thousand that escaped mutilation in 1955 worked the 1957 football season, and they've moldered in mothballs ever since.

Surplus garments in a London warehouse led to another brief fashion fad in 1958. David Seiniger of New York's Empire Imports stumbled on a cache of bobbies' capes during a British buying trip. The capes were the oilskin rainy-day uniforms worn by the bobbies on state occasions, and each came complete with an official badge. Seiniger brought 2,000 home, sold them in Manhattan as capes and skirts, and imported 8,000 more, along with 5,000 official helmets. Word of the sales, however, leaked in London, and created a public outcry. Blooming American women were wearing bloody bobbies' badges! End of British export, end of craze.

Controversy of a different sort surrounded another fashion fad a dozen years before. The bikini had appeared on French beaches as early as 1946, shocking even the chic European sun-worshippers. It arrived in the United States in 1948, a skimpy flag of sexual revolution, or so it seemed to the self-appointed protectors of our spiritual virginity—who were soon to suffer the unkindest cut from an unexpected quarter.

That same year, Dr. Alfred C. Kinsey, a little-known biologist, published *Sexual Behavior in the Human Male*; the companion volume on the female followed in 1953. The reports were based on interviews with a test group of 16,500 men, women, and children, and for the first time the sexually confused, guilty, or misinformed—which included just about everybody—knew they were not alone.

During the following decade, "post office" and "spin-the-bottle" became, quite literally, kid stuff—standard fare at grade-school parties when the grown-ups weren't around. Teen-agers had already moved on to richer experimentation. Simple necking, or getting to "first base," was easy; heavier petting at "second" or "third base," less so. And for the benchwarmers who dreamed of the day they would get into the game, maybe even hit a home run, a furtive perusal of the new popular literature, undergoing its own sexual awakening, provided plenty of pointers.

In 1947, Mike Hammer splattered onto the scene with *I, the Jury*, written in nine days. Mickey Spillane's subsequent books each sold upwards of one million copies of killer prose: "She was there in my arms again, softly at first and hungry-mouthed again. Her fingers were velvet cat-claws, kneading me gently, searching and finding."

In 1951, Sergeant Warden had the captain's wife on the beach in *From Here to Eternity*; five years later, Rodney had humiliation—but not Betty—on the back seat in *Peyton Place*; and in the rehabilitated 1928 classic, Lady Chatterly had John Thomas everywhere. The kids read them all, at least the dirty parts, and for more clinical advice turned to Dr. Eustace Chesser's *Love Without Fear*. That primitive sex manual first appeared in 1947, and by the mid-1950's, dog-eared, yellowing copies that flipped open automatically to "Painful Pleasures" and "the kiss of love" were stashed in the dark corners of high-school lockers from coast to coast.

For those who bemoaned the degeneracy of American youth, it was a mere hop from "those books" to creeping immorality, a short skip from there to juvenile delinquency. And that noise called rock 'n' roll, they wailed, was nurturing it all.

The term was coined by disc jockey Alan Freed in 1952 to describe the sound that was drowning out the crooners and the sticky sentimentality of Rosemary Clooney and Patti Page. The "Big Beat" didn't get off the ground, however, until 1954 when Bill Haley and The Comets recorded "Rock Around the Clock," a hit that would sell 16 million copies by the end of the decade, and an estimated 25 million to date. It was the best-selling pop single ever issued, but as an indication of how gradually the kids were latching on to a musical form that was distinctly theirs, Perry Como was still their king two years later: a 1956 survey of teenagers' favorite vocalists put Como first, Elvis second. Nevertheless, Elvis' "Heartbreak Hotel" was that summer's runaway best seller, and he became the center of the rock 'n' roll phenomenon, *the* pop music fad of the decade.

Surprisingly, rock did not immediately inspire an accompanying set of new dances. When Dick Clark's "American Bandstand" began broadcasting from Philadelphia in 1957, we watched for endless hours as our favorite couples performed muted variations of the Jitterbug and shuffled through the nondance that has come to characterize America's response to the ballad. Weddings, bar mitzvahs, and high-school proms included the obligatory Bunny Hop; the Stroll, a smooth, sensual glide punctuated by hand-clapping, was a rock 'n' roll variation of the Virginia Reel, and a brief rage around 1958. But the profusion of rock 'n' roll dances would wait until the 1960's and the legacy of the Twist, the first major pop dance without body contact.

For the ballroom dancing set, Latin music was the major influence of the era. Across the nation Arthur Murray's dance studios kept us wiggling to the latest Latin rhythms: the Conga, Samba, and Tango in the late 1940's; the Cha-Cha, Mambo, and Merengue of the mid-1950's.

When they weren't walking down lonely street to Heartbreak Hotel, or finding their thrill on Blueberry Hill, cleancut middle-class kids told "grape jokes," drew "droodles," and hung out at the neon-lit fast-food drive-ins that popped up along America's main drags faster than pimples on a pubescent face. If they managed to obtain a phony I.D. and chug-a-lug a few brews, they spent the ride home "mooning" the squares in neighboring vehicles. Bare buttocks exposed through a side window in a "flying moon" were worth three points in New York suburbs; the more treacherous "standing moon," flashed while stopped at a red light, scored five.

The college students of the 1950's have been called "The Silent Generation." Crew-cutted, page-boyed, Bermuda-shorted, these were kids without politics, without social conscience, and without passions greater than football, fraternity hazing, and sex. In the saturnalian spring season, the air would vibrate with the guarded sexual signals of the panty raid, generally greeted with equal enthusiasm by the raiders and the raided. College officials gave them mixed reviews, and resident psychologists, well-versed in their Kinsey, nodded their heads sagely. A few panty raids escalated into full-scale riots. Extensive property damage and hysterical coeds dragged half-dressed and screaming from their dorms brought the arrival of local police armed with tear gas. But these were the exceptions. The rule was a harmless shower of bras, panties, and cold water descending upon the hordes of the horny.

In 1955 collegians discovered the pleasure of stuffing themselves into automobiles. The fad died quickly, but was resurrected four years later as a logical extension of the phone booth stuffing madness. Nineteen fifty-nine is also remembered as the year of the "hunker." Restricted almost exclusively to Southern and Midwestern institutions of higher learning, "hunkering" was a form of

111

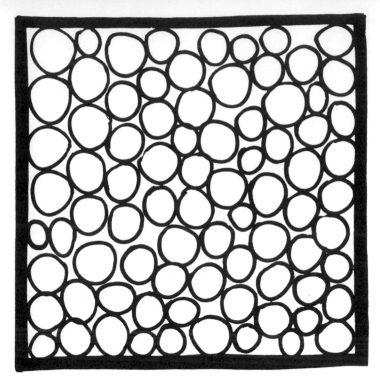

*Spare eyes for Little Orphan Annie.*

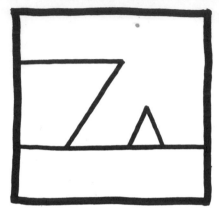

*A ship arriving too late
to save a drowning witch.*

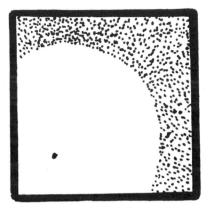

*Germs avoiding friend
who has caught penicillin.*

Droodles were the rage in the early 1950's, the
brainchild of funnyman Roger Price. Easy to
draw, they invited leaps of creativity from comics
of all ages. Above and opposite, some of Price's
pungent prototypes.

"sociable squatting" on one's haunches, the term itself probably
deriving from the Scottish "hunkers" for haunches. One hunkered
while studying and watching television; one hunkered by way of
participating in the exciting enterprise of creating new forms.
Thus, the "outside hunker" with arms outside the knees; the "inside hunker" with arms. . . . It is believed that the art originated in
the Ozarks where mountain people so squatted to avoid a lapful of
wood shavings while they whittled. But even that practical an ob-
jective appears to be absent from the design of the dedicated
students at the University of Arkansas and other participating·
schools. They, one must conclude, hunkered for the hell of it.

We also, it would seem, hula-hooped for the hell of it, though
unconscious eroticism, the security suggested by encirclement,
rebellion—all these and more were offered as explanations for the

*Eiffel Tower as seen by guard in armored truck.*

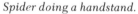

*Three degrees below zero.*

*Spider doing a handstand.*

*The outside world as seen by a little man living in a beer can.*

basic appeal of the remarkably simple toy that became, in 1958, an international *cause célèbre*. Outlawed in Japan, ridiculed by the Russians as an example of the "emptiness of American culture," in five months' the hula hoop raked in twice the sum disbursed by the State Department for cultural educational exchange programs during the entire year.

In 1957 a visiting Australian had mentioned his countrymen's use of bamboo hoops as a gym class exercise to two young Californians, Richard Knerr and Arthur "Spud" Melin. Founders of the Wham-O Manufacturing Company of San Gabriel, they were doing a modest business in slingshots, boomerangs, and other athletic esoterica, and decided to take the tip from their friend from down under. They set to work solving the problem of determining the best "hoop-to-waist" ratio, and introduced the result in

*Above, Milton Berle sashays through one of the gag acts that made him King of Television in the 1950s. "Uncle Miltie" was deposed in the next decade, but during his heyday, the water pressure in key Midwestern cities shot up when he made his weekly TV appearances: The fans sat glued to the tube, forsaking even a trip to the john.*

Pasadena playgrounds. According to Knerr, their plastic hoop had the longest "play value" of any toy they had ever produced. Somewhat unprepared for the international success that awaited the hula hoop, the Wham-O duo found themselves unable to police their patent, and soon "Spin-a-hoop," "Hoop-d-do" and some forty other American varieties were competing for their share of international sales of between 60 million and 100 million hoops in 1958. In November, when *The Wall Street Journal* announced HOOPS HAVE HAD IT, toy manufacturers, $45 million richer, had no complaints. Wham-O, convinced that the future was in fads, set out on the elusive search for another biggie.

As with so many other fad mongers of the 1950's, hoop hucksters had received free promotional reinforcement from the mass media, particularly television. The medium was a little over ten years old now and had made remarkable strides in selling to us, informing us, amusing us. In 1948 fewer than 2 percent of American homes had TV sets, but "Howdy Doody" was already on the air, as were "Meet the Press" and Chiquita Banana. Professional wrestling and roller derby were early TV fads, used as filler between big league baseball games and boxing matches. Movie box-office revenues were plunging and the film industry was running scared. The studios tried 3-D and Cinerama, Cinemascope and Smell-O-Vision, but TV was entering its golden age, and with few exceptions Hollywood was left to bang its head against a solid wall of Berle and Lucy, Caesar and Coca, Sergeant Friday and Sergeant Bilko, Lawrence Welk and "Playhouse 90."

In 1959, 86 percent of us had a TV set, and the average American spent forty-two hours a week watching it. In that final summer of the 1950's, the airwaves sizzled with the quiz-show scandals, and the $64,000 question was, did they or didn't they fix Patty Duke? In a dozen years TV had taken us from wrestler Gorgeous George, brawny and wholesome, to Professor Charles Van Doren, brainy and corrupt. The images had all flashed before us. Never before had the events of a decade been so sharply etched on our collective memory. Perhaps that's why, in another dozen years, when we longed to escape from other scandals, other disgraces, the Fabulous Fifties came so quickly and vividly to mind and became, themselves, a fad.

*The winner and new Bubbly Champ, Philadelphia, 1947.*

## Big, Bigger, Bang!

Bigger was best in the postwar years, and the most inflatable commodity around was bubble gum. Its invention in the late 1920's is credited to Walter E. Diemar of the Fleer Corporation, and by the 1940's it had been perfected to the limits of elasticity. The penny price also doubled, kicking off preteen protest marches in 1946. But even with the inflated price of the goods, bubble-gum-blowing contests became a national fad in 1947, and eventually a national institution.

*Diemar and bubble, 1967.*

*Cleveland winner, above;
also-rans, below, 1947.*

*Bubble gum, baseball, and a California Little Leaguer in a classic symbiotic relationship, 1954.*

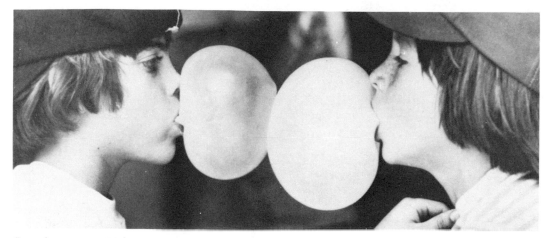

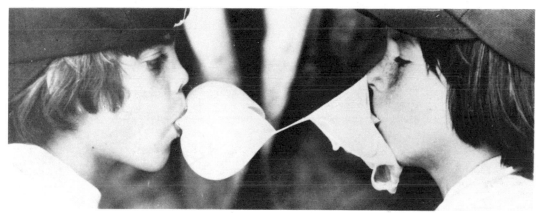

*Complications in Melrose, Mass., 1976.*

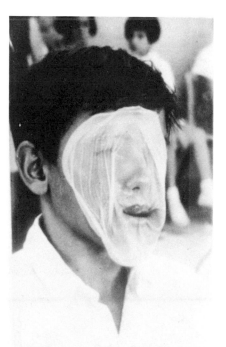

*Louisville blowout, 1968.*

*San Jose, California.*

## TOGETHER ON CAMPUS

To wit: twenty-three Memphis State Sigma Kappas, opposite, plus booster, together in a campus phone booth; twenty-one Lamda Chi Alphas (bottom), plus mascot, together in an Austin-Healy; they were nine, going for ten, in a California phone booth, right, when the cops blew the whistle. Below, a victimized pharmacy student together with the *Newark News*.

*April Fool's Day, 1959.*

*Rutgers, above;*
*Franklin & Marshall, below, 1959.*

*Boys, together with panties, University of Illinois, Spring 1953.*

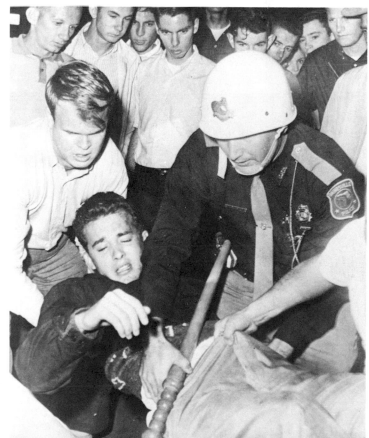

*Opposite: Tufts, together with Jackson College, Spring, 1952. At right, panty raider together with the Florida law.*

*The agony of ecstasy; Elvis
hits Philadelphia, April 1957.*

## "THAT'S ALL RIGHT, MAMA" AND AFTER

It started in 1954 with a couple of nice, lively
tunes he wrote himself and recorded privately
for his Mums on the occasion of her birthday.
The recording engineer liked the sound and a
couple of months later invited him back to cut a
single called "That's All Right, Mama." A Memphis disc jockey gave it a twirl, and when the
orders rolled in—6,000 in one week in Memphis
alone—it appeared the boy had something. Elvis
didn't know what it was, he said sometime later,
"but I don't want it never to end."

*Sonny with Dads and Mums;*
*down home, 1956.*

*"A mild-mannered country kid,"*
Steve Allen said of him.
*"Not too bright, perhaps, but sincere."*

*"Love me tender," he warbled. "We do," came the response from Hollywood, above, to Times Square, below.*

*"I tell you flatly, he can't last," said Jackie Gleason back in 1956. But two decades later, Elvis fans (see overleaf) were still legion.*

*August 1977, and four leftover Elvis fans join the line outside their hero's mausoleum in Memphis, Tennessee. Elvis died on Tuesday, August 16; in the weeks that followed, commemorative T-shirts like those above went on sale the world over, the last fad to spin off the career of the fading star who had given rock 'n' roll its style two decades before.*

*L. Ron Hubbard—Dianetics then; Scientology today.*

## MIND AND BODY IN THE NIFTY FIFTIES

Dudley LeBlanc, Louisiana state senator, put the cure to everything in a Hadacol bottle; Gaylord Hauser hawked youth in his best seller, *Look Younger, Live Longer*—and made blackstrap molasses a national fad. In *his* best seller, *Dianetics, the Modern Science of Mental Health*, former sci-fi writer L. Ron Hubbard hawked an engram-free existence. You could get "clear" of those nasty psychological scars with a dianetics therapist, only twenty-five bucks an hour in those halcyon days.

*Which Twin has the Toni?*

*The first Toni Twins—
beauty in a home perm bottle, 1947.*

*Gaylord Hauser, left, had us mired in molasses in 1950, searching for "youthful years" and a cure for baldness. Dudley LeBlanc, above, moved two million bottles of Hadacol a month during its 1950 peak—each with as much booze as a double martini. We felt no pain.*

The 1950's brought roller skating back—this time as a chilling, thrilling spectator sport that filled thousands of hours of television time. Above, eight padded derbyists get ready, get set, GO! Below, a chilling, thrilling spill.

Bowling was big in the Nifty Fifties—
the *national sport for the crewcut set.*
At right, a strike, 1957.

For most of us in the Fabulous Fifties, there was no sport quite like
hula hooping. At left, Dick Gillespie
who, in 1958, was the first person
to climb in and find out if it could
be done. It could: see overleaf.

*A Benedictine convent, Oklahoma City.*

*Tokyo*

*Los Angeles*

*Indianapolis*

*Weisbaden, West Germany*

# "We Shall Overcome" 1960-1976

It was the Fourth of July 1976 and the United States was two hundred years old. Uncle Sam was decked out in his top hat, his red Fonzie T-shirt, and his blue and white bleached jeans. His skateboard was fiberglass, his CB radio was double-band, and his smile was self-satisfied: his est training had paid off, and he had survived—survived sixteen years of assassinations, ghetto and campus riots, antiwar demonstrations, political scandal, and protest marches by a dazzling spectrum of special interest groups. The lexicon of crisis had filled with new names: John Kennedy, Oswald, and Ruby; Robert Kennedy and Sirhan Sirhan; Martin Luther King and James Earl Ray; the Berrigans and Spock; Savo and Rudd; Newton, Cleaver, and Carmichael; Lieutenant Calley; Steinem and Freidan; Cesar Chavez; Nixon, the "plumbers," and the "palace guard." But when the world was too much with us, we still had Tiny Tim.

We had Tiny Tim, and Bogie and Batman, Steppenwolf and Mick Jaggar, Che, Mary Hartman and the Reverend Moon —had all our fads because we needed them.

Fads are elusive phenomena, rather like certain mysterious atomic particles that nuclear physicists observe. Apparently trivial, random particles, they pop in and out of view without discernible rhyme or reason. But the physicist knows that something can't spring from nothing, and assumes the existence of invisible, subatomic motivation. Fads don't spring out of a

*"Yucch," she said, emerging from a mud bath at the University of Miami in 1967. Her reaction typified, for most of us, our feelings about the decade itself. For a lineup of famous fault-finders, see overleaf.*

*Friedan: anti-sexist-pig.*

*Chavez: anti-non-union grapes.*

vacuum either. They come as messengers, bearing witness to invisible strata of human life—and speaking, for the most part, in
tongues.

In the 1960's and 1970's, the very coincidence of so many fads
bespeaks of the trauma of our times; and some of those fads speak
of specific traumas. The 1973 fad, for example, of wearing de-
signer John Kloss's inexpensive nightgowns as evening dresses into
some of Manhattan's more expensive watering holes. An oblique
response to the runaway inflation we suffered that summer, it
couldn't have happened during a time of easy money.

With other fads, particularly those of certain cultural sub-
groups, it's a timeless desire that's the motive. In 1966, thousands
of teen-agers wore German Iron Crosses, the Nazi emblem first
popularized here by California's Hell's Angels. From the motorcy-
cle cultists the crosses spread to West Coast surfers, and then to
the teen-agers, who made them "the hottest single novelty item in
years," according to the Rhode Island manufacturer whose plant
turned out 24,000 a day. The crosses, however, expressed not
neo-Nazism, but the desire, endemic to adolescence, to outrage

Ginsberg: anti-war.

Rudd: anti.

adult authority. "It really upsets your parents," said one Los Angeles high-school student. "That's why everyone buys them."

Teen-agers love fads. Trapped between childhood and adult-hood, they form a closed society of their own, embracing the emblems of music, dance, fashion, and slang fads that make them look, sound, and act different from everyone else. The more extravagant the emblem, the less likely the fad will be imitated; and the more outrageously inimitable it is, the more kids love it.

The isolation teen-agers seek in a fad doesn't always last though. In 1964, two years before they donned their Iron Crosses, teen-agers discovered The Beatles. To the shock of the adult crowd, they bought Beatles buttons, wigs, wallets, and wallpaper, copied their shaggy haircuts, and revered the repetitive simplicity of such early Beatles lyrics as "She loves you, yeah, yeah, yeah." Their reverence was worth $50 million in 1964 alone.

At an early point in the explosion, sociologist David Reisman identified Beatlemania as "a form of protest against the adult world." But it wouldn't last, he went on to say. "Compared to the Elvis Presley craze it is a very minor one." Not only did Reisman

139

make the mistake of predicting the duration of a fad before it had peaked—a treacherous endeavor—he couldn't foresee that Beatlemania would spread far beyond teen-agers, that the boys from Liverpool would be recognized as major innovators, cornerstones of the popular music of our era.

More astonishing, The Beatles accomplished that without losing their teen fans. The ability to find acceptance in the larger world without losing the following of those first hardcore fans is typical only of the fads, of whatever origin, that become part of mainstream American culture. But it is particularly atypical of the fads that pop up out of the teen-age strata: generally, teen-agers drop their fads as soon as other age groups invade. Consider, for example, the Twist.

Originated by Hank Ballard in 1959 and adopted by teen-agers all across the country, the Twist turned into a big business proposition with Chubby Checker's 1961 recording and TV demonstrations. Discotheques like Arthur's and the Peppermint Lounge opened to provide Twisting arenas, and by 1962, Twisters could

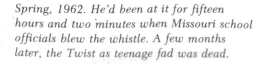

*Spring, 1962. He'd been at it for fifteen hours and two minutes when Missouri school officials blew the whistle. A few months later, the Twist as teenage fad was dead.*

*August 24, 1964. The Beatles hit the Hollywood Bowl. Stunned, a parent hopes it will pass. It didn't.*

buy special shoes, shirts, wallets, pajamas, cufflinks, candy, and a "Twisteroo" fur-trimmed cap. A clerk at Gimbel's New York store explained that "anything with fringe sells to twisters," including a peppermint-striped fringed dress for $5.99, an assortment of fringed belts from $1.25 to $4.99, and a fifty-nine-cent fringed garter.

With that, the teen-agers simply gave it up. In Washington, D.C., the last straw had already come with Jackie Kennedy's White House Twist party. Nationwide, the kids took up new forms, the Frug, the Monkey, the Watusi and Hully-Gully, the Slop, Swim, Jerk, Fly, Pony, and Mashed Potato, abandoning each one when adult cafe society got the knack of it.

A good many of those grown-ups learned the steps from "Killer Joe" Piro. A dancing instructor who made his fortune at the round of political and society parties in the early 1960's, Killer Joe was eventually hired by the Schenley liquor concern to create a dance they called the Mule. The plan was to promote it along with their new vodka drink of the same name. But the kids wouldn't be caught dead dancing that Madison Avenue hokum, and the adults danced only what the kids did. The Mule never budged.

*Atlantic City, six days later. The Beatles fever is rising. It lasted as long as they did, dying only when they went their separate ways in 1970. We wanted, John said, "to be bigger than Elvis." And they were.*

Perhaps the only thing kids invented faster than dances in the 1960's was argot. Baby-sitting was "the bawl game" for 1965 teens, carrying your lunch to school was "brown-bagging it," and bizarre behavior was "off the wall." By 1966 "cool," so used up as to be uncool, had been replaced by "boss," "tough," "groovy," "bitchin'," and the superlative "outta *sight!*"

Lexicographers know that the function of slang is secrecy: it makes you literally incomprehensible to outsiders. Thus most teen-age slang remains local, for once it's deciphered by adults it's usually dropped by the kids before it can flower nationally. In 1968, high school students in Cheyenne, Wyoming, called guitars "boxes," immature peers were "bubble-gummers," and convertible cars were "rag tops." Success was "lucking out," ending a relationship was "hanging it up," and concentrated thinking was "using your Clyde." "Lucking out" snuck by and did go national, but the kids of Cheyenne dropped the rest as soon as "they" discovered them.

Fashion fads will occasionally keep the grown-ups at bay, too, particularly if the fad is outrageously silly. In 1965, girls in Versailles, Kentucky, bought the biggest, gaudiest dime-store rings they could find. Boys in southern California wore glassless eyeglasses. The next year kids in Orlando, Florida, were making rings by filing down the necks of Coke bottles; teen-agers in Salt Lake City were wearing their sunglasses upside down. By the mid-1970's, it was mood rings whose stones changed color with the disposition of the bearer, and necklaces made of plastic tubing that glowed an unforgettable, gaudy neon in broad daylight. Both met the basic criteria: they were cheap to acquire, easy to get rid of should the world catch on, and highly visible routes to the prestige and security of being "in."

Security comes, too, from inclusion in a group that excludes. Middle-class kids of the late 1960's wore the jeans, denim shirts, and work boots of the "working class," both to identify themselves with the supporters of, for instance, Cesar Chavez and the migrant farmworkers, and to exclude themselves from the "burned-out bourgeois world" of their parents.

Similarly in the case of D. B. Cooper, antibourgeois antihero of 1971. On Thanksgiving eve, D. B. hijacked a Northwest Orient jet, parachuted away with $200,000 in ransom money, and disappeared in the mountains somewhere between Seattle and Reno. Seventy-two hours later, to the disgust of Northwest Orient Airlines, assorted citizens' groups, and the pilots' union, Western teen-agers were buying T-shirts that read "D. B. Cooper, where are you?" and a record about the new dropout hero was soon on its way up the pop music charts. There was no mistaking the message: as far as the kids were concerned, D. B. had discovered the best way to fly.

But teen-agers, whatever else they may be, are human, and some teen-age fashion fads spring from emotional sources common to all of us. There was, for instance, the granny dress that became a teen-age craze in 1965. Grannies first appeared in Los Angeles— charming, nostalgic, and handmade. (After *Women's Wear Daily* picked up on the fad, mass-produced models rolled across the prairies to the Eastern frontier, at which point they disappeared from California: "When anyone can walk into a department store and buy a granny dress," sniffed one young lady from Los Angeles, "we drop them quick.") Some reports suggested the original California models were inspired by the ankle-length frontier dresses worn by Disneyland employees; others said they were a defiant response to a local TV dance-show host who had chided the kids about their distractingly short short-skirts. But whatever the stimulus, their appeal was romance. They were pretty, and they were sexy.

All of us like to feel sexy. In the summer of 1965, teen-agers cut up their shoes and sneakers to create an "air-conditioned" and, they decided, sexy look. In Florida, Michigan, and Massachusetts, the textured stockings that accompanied miniskirts were dropped in favor of home-made knee designs, created with watercolors or paste-on cutouts of butterflies and flowers. In New Jersey, teen-age girls used acrylics to paint brightly colored sandals and thongs on their bare feet. Princess Grace herself turned up with golden lacework painted across her imperial brow, and eventually thousands of American females from teenyboppers on up were adorning shoulders, waists, thighs, cheeks, eyelids, and earlobes with designs of their own devising. Painting all of the body was the next logical step. We took that one too.

The sexy fad almost died out in 1970, but returned shortly thereafter with a new wrinkle: real tattoos.

Tattoo parlors were, and still are, illegal in many cities, but women seek out master tattoo artists like Lyle Tuttle and Spider Webb anyway, forsaking decals, marker pens, and watercolors for the nearly painless pleasures of the electric needle. Clearly the permanence of a shoulder butterfly or a buttock rose makes the wearer feel daring, special, and awfully sexy.

In tattoo faddists of all ages was something that loved the exhibitionism of it—that loved the shocked, even hostile stares of those for whom the tattoos, like any exotic fad, signalled change and thus a threat. And something in them that loved the solemn stories featured in *Time* and *Newsweek* and their local papers.

Virtually every fad is, in some measure, exhibitionistic; and every faddist enjoys, in some measure, being on exhibition—from the estimated three thousand topless bathing suit faddists of the 1960's to the backgammon faddists of the 1970's, who didn't, in fact, do anything very extraordinary but did it in such very extraordinary numbers that the rest of us, along with the national media, had to watch.

But no one has been so consistently exhibitionistic as the stunt-prone college student. Take, for starters, those who indulged in the piano-wrecking fad we imported in 1963. A six-man team of student engineers at England's Derby College of Technology, working with such hand tools as axes, sledgehammers, crowbars, and brooms, were the first to discover the joys of demolishing a piano and passing its pieces through a small hole. Their time was a bare fourteen-plus minutes. At Cal Tech, where the fad began its American run, competitors organized a "Piano Reduction Study Group," which proclaimed its desire "to reduce the piano, in the shortest possible time, to such a state that it may be passed through an aperture of 20 centimeters in diameter." One Cal Tech team turned in a time of 10 minutes, 44.4 seconds. That record was overturned by the wrecking crew from Wayne State. They did it in a smashing 4 minutes, 51 seconds.

It's almost irresistible to guess that piano-wrecking was faddish among engineering students because it represented a mock assault on the arts, whose spokesmen have not always been kind to tech-

Tattoos: national fad, 1973.

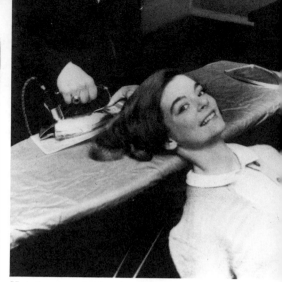
Hair ironing: high school fad, 1964.

nologists, particularly in our era. But most college fads don't spin out of such socio-cultural complexities. Most college fads are the primal scream of kids reacting to the timeless pressures of taking exams and making "career choices."

"Gronking," for instance, a 1965 fad, *was* a primal scream. Students simply banded together and screamed "GRONNNK" at the top of their lungs. That was all, but gronking echoed across our Eastern campuses—particularly at exam time.

Other students have found other release valves. In 1961 they conducted telephone talkathons and bed-pushing marathons; in 1962 at Emory University and neighboring Southern schools, they "heubished"—fraternity brothers, in boredom assembled, taking long, hot spins in the giant clothes dryers manufactured by the Heubish company.

At Colorado State, the men of Sigma Chi found their 1967 sweetheart in parachute riding: you sat, perhaps stood, on a piece of heavy cardboard pulled along the grass by a wind-filled chute at speeds of up to 30 miles per hour. At Harvard in 1973, students did the goldfish swallowers of 1939 one better. Sophomore full-back Jay Bennett and an understandably limited number of others began to eat the university's light bulbs. The bulbs were carefully broken, chewed one shard at a time into a fine powder, and swallowed with salad dressing or crunchy granola. When quizzed about their preference for brands and wattage, the students were admirably open-minded. "I eat whatever the university uses," said one.

*T-p'ing: college fad, 1964.*

In 1966, mock murder had been the release at, among·other centers of learning, Oberlin, the Illinois Institute of Technology, and the University of Chicago. In "The Hunt Game," based on the plot of the film *The Tenth Victim*, students played cat-and-mouse during four-day sessions. Fictional "kills," scored on the basis of ingenuity and skill of execution, were accomplished by flashlight "laser beams," rubber-band "high voltage wires," and similar substitutes for the deadly real thing. One student received a notice on the letterhead of the school finance office that began with standard fare about tuition charges. It concluded, "By the way, you have just been handling paper impregnated with contact poison— phenylhydrazine substitution products. This poison should by now be spreading through your system and you will lie groaning on the floor. This is your hunter speaking. You are now dead."

At Chicago, the game's initiators described it not only as "a means of letting off aggression, a way to break some of the academic tension on campus" but "a good way to meet girls." At Oberlin, the last goal was perfected: hunters and victims, generally of opposite sexes, were paired by an IBM computer, a sociable application of technology inspired by the computer dating fad that had been punch-carding romance into American campuses for the past several months.

The brainchild of Harvard classmates Jeff Tarr and Voughn Morrill, Operation Match was, announced *Mademoiselle*, "the biggest American fad since the hula hoop." Its success was not universally applauded, the media poignantly editorializing about the technological depersonalization of, at long last, even love.

For several years the campuses simmered, with little time for faddish diversion. But when the protest dust finally settled, America was merrily scandalized by the most extraordinary fad in memory. It was 1974, and the streakers had arrived.

During the six weeks from late January to mid-March, they blazed across the very same pages of national magazines and newspapers that carried the story of the Nixon impeachment inquiry. They streaked the Lyndon Johnson Library, making Lady Bird laugh and Walter Cronkite blush. They streaked through police stations and the Michigan legislature. They streaked around West Point, and through student-government meetings where the issue was the streaker problem. They streaked the Academy Awards ceremony, and a literary cocktail party at New York's St. Regis Hotel. They streaked by parachute, in 20-below weather, in wheelchairs, and on unicycles. After they streaked through an Atlanta bus, the driver was asked if they were male or female. "I couldn't tell," he replied. "They were wearing masks."

Records were broken and rebroken daily. When it was over, longest streak honors went to Texas Tech students who skittered about for five hours. The University of Georgia mustered 1,543 students for the largest streak. Laura Barton, a freshman at Carlton College in Minnesota, became the first female streaker when she appeared for an unscheduled curtain call following the school production of *Measure for Measure*. Ms. Barton won fame, but lost her boyfriend, a straight-laced fellow she was probably well rid of.

A few students were arrested, and two states tried and failed to make streaking a crime. But most college administrators considered it all a welcome change from the days of campus riots and bombings. As *Newsweek* observed, it was "the sort of totally absurd phenomenon the nation needed after a winter of lousy news."

Diversionary and splendid as it all was, streaking was quintessentially and, with only a few exceptions, collegiate: if you weren't stabled at a campus, chances were you didn't bother to give it a try. In 1973, on the other hand, when Elizabeth Taylor showed up at Hollywood parties wearing a puka shell necklace from her brother Howard, tens of thousands of us bothered. The movie crowd was knocked out, puka shells got very hot, and by the fall of 1974, fashionable boutiques in California and Hawaii were getting as much as $150 for the baubles that sold for $6 a year earlier.

Fad upon fad spins out of our emulation of celebrities, from Jack Kennedy's rocking chairs and Jackie's pillbox hats to Gloria Steinem's blond-streaked hair and aviator glasses. Occasionally, as in the Spiro Agnew watch fad of 1969, it works the other way around. While some of the Agnew watches were, in fact, purchased by those who considered Spiro their hero, the association with the Mickey Mouse watch boom of two years earlier wasn't lost on the rest of us. Most of the watches circled the wrists of the enemy—those "nattering nabobs of negativity" who had invoked the vice-presidential wrath.

Watergate gave us ridicule fads too: a Watergate game, the wanted posters featuring Nixon's rogues gallery, and the T-shirts, sweatshirts, and buttons calling for impeachment. Nixon and the "palace guard" having been done in, a new literary fad gripped us: novels, "nonfiction" novels, and unadulterated nonfiction by and about the antiheroes of Watergate topped best-seller lists and publishers' revenue sheets.

But no group of celebrities—hero or antihero—has given us as many fads as the rock stars. Even their fans spawn fads: when British teenyboppers took to the "total look" of high boots, white stockings, straight hair, Liverpool cap, and micro-mini skirt, American teenyboppers took, too.

For teen-age boys, the models were the British rock stars themselves. Their "mod" uniforms, initially worn for on-stage theatrical effect, were flamboyant and flashy and decadent. But soon their Chelsea boots and Dutch-boy caps and ornate silk shirts were copied for street dress; and when these elaborate trappings arrived here, the revolution was on. British and American rock stars alike began finding their hallmarks reproduced by the thousands. Jim McGuinn, lead guitarist of The Byrds, wore tiny tinted "Ben Franklin" glasses to protect his eyes from the stage lights; the kids started wearing them because McGuinn did. The Rolling Stones wore plaid and checked pants; Sonny and Cher

149

wore hip-hugger belts; Paul Revere and The Raiders wore paisley shirts and leather vests; Herman's Hermits wore round-toed boots—so the kids wore plaid pants with hip-hugger belts and paisley shirts with leather vests, and everybody wore round-toed boots. For by then, the fads that had trickled down from rock star to rock fan had trickled up to dad himself, corporation man and come-lately long hair.

But however quick we are to take our fads from the backs of rock stars, movie stars, first ladies, and the high school set, nothing can create a national fad quite as fast as a national crisis. In 1967 at the height of the Vietnam war, *Quotations from Chairman Mao Tse-tung* became a national best seller nearly overnight: by March, even Brentano's branch at the Pentagon had sold one thousand copies, and in Manhattan, the Chairman's wisdom was quoted at cocktail parties as glibly as Confucius' sayings had been at the high-school malt shop a quarter-century before. In 1972, Nixon's visit to Peking brought a flood of Chinese crafts and clothes, a third American Ping-Pong renaissance—and inspiration to New York promoter Stanley Weston. Deciding to chance a ride on the wave of Chinaphilia, Weston purchased all rights to the Charlie Chan character and began to promote Charlie Chan Chinese foods, an animated TV series, comic strips, paperback books, and a Broadway show. But the necessary development time for such ventures would prove greater than our interest, Oriental-Americans who viewed Chan as a Chinese "Uncle Tom" threatened to boycott, and in the end, Weston wished he'd read his fortune cookies more carefully.

Sometimes a fad seems almost to stumble to life, taking even its promoter by surprise. There is, for instance, the case of Donald F. Duncan, Jr., son of the entrepreneur who in 1929 had given the Filipino weapon-turned-toy the name "yo-yo." In 1961, Duncan, Jr. was sitting on top of 90 percent of a sluggish yo-yo market when he shifted his crack Filipino demonstration team from live neighborhood performances to TV kiddy shows. Within weeks yo-yos were spinning wildly through Salt Lake City, Wichita, Kansas City, Memphis, Birmingham, and Nashville. In New York, authorized retailers and a lively troop of black market regulars sold an estimated 4 million in eight weeks. Back in Nashville, population 322,000, Duncan sold 350,000 in two months.

The yo-yo king sold a total of 15 million in 1961, but Duncan misjudged the very nature of his sales. "We don't want this to become a mad fad like the hula hoop," he said. "We want to keep it going." It couldn't be done. As Wham-O vice president Robert Payne would point out ten years later, producers of fad products deal "with different consumer motivations, a different kind of marketing." Most fad products now last only a few months, according to a 1971 *Business Week* report. Their lives begin with a dramatic burst of sales, but they end with a bang and a market saturated with imitations. The key is to produce fast, market fast, through as many channels as possible, and then move on, preferably to a new fad.

Wham-O did all of that with Super Ball. The stuff of Super Balls had been created in 1963 by rubber chemist Norman Stingley during spare-time experimentation in high-resiliency synthetics. The ball he developed had a 92 percent "recovery rate"—sufficient bounce to keep it moving for about a minute a drop. Compared to the ten-second bounce life of a new tennis ball, that was spectacular. The stuff kept falling apart, but two years of research with Wham-O fixed that, and in 1965 they flooded the market with Super Ball. Though the madness lasted less than a year, Wham-O sold millions of balls, and moved on in its happy search for new fish to fry. Silly String came next, and eventually Frisbees.

Advertising copywriters, by dint of occupation, seem to know intuitively what Wham-O knows. In 1961, San Francisco copywriter Howard Gossage was in the midst of writing a beer commercial when he came up with the idea of sweatshirts bearing the images of Beethoven, Bach, and Brahms. He licensed the designs to Philadelphia's Eagle Shirtmakers, who sold sixty thousand at $4 apiece—undoubtedly helped in some small measure by Van Cliburn, who bought Brahms, Arthur Fiedler, who bought Beethoven, and diplomatic Leonard Bernstein, who bought all three.

Then there was the trio of Chicago copywriters who conceived the Executive Coloring Book in late 1961, decided on an initial print order of 1,600 books, and eleven months later had sold three hundred thousand at $2.98 a clip. The market filled up with the predictable imitators: the JFK Coloring Book, the Nikita Khrushchev Coloring Book, and a spate of others spoofing the

United Nations, bartenders, psychiatrists, corporations, and the John Birch Society. By October 1962, one million adult coloring books had been sold. Crayon sales hadn't budged an inch, of course. "I am a patient," read one caption in the Psychiatric Coloring Book. "My analyst says I am confused and abstract. Color me confused and abstract."

Another copywriter, Gary Dahl of Los Altos, California, was having a few with the boys one night in early 1975 when the conversation turned to pets. Dahl listened to tales of cats, dogs, hamsters, and finally launched into an impromptu discourse about his rock. Obedient. Loyal. Clean. No upkeep at all. The guys loved it.

According to Don Kracke, West Coast writer and inventor, Dahl went home and turned out the Pet Rock training manual— planning the carrying box, the excelsior packing, even the rock itself as little more than props to support a short, funny book. Dahl also made the wise and, Kracke notes, unusual decision that retail price and production, distribution, and promotion costs had to be structured so he would personally net $1 per pet sold. He organized a crack distribution team, geared up for the 1975 Christmas season, and moved—quick, before the rip-offs could make it to the Christmas market. Instinctively, Dahl did all the right things. As a result, Kracke points out, he is now the richest man in Los Altos, California.

The competition that Dahl managed to stave off, however, can be advantageous. Therein lies one secret to the success of Fuzzy Foot. A "fun fur" rug in the shape of a giant paw, Fuzzy Foot bombed when it was introduced in 1968. The manufacturers, Glenoit Mills, tried again, cautiously, in 1970. When they sold 1,500 rugs in two and a half days at the Hecht Company department store in Washington, D.C., Glenoit president Clarence Hafford smelled money and mobilized his forces.

Interviews with Hecht's executives and sales staff were conducted "as a starter," Hafford told *Business Week* in August 1971. Then, said another company executive, "we went into competition with ourselves by supplying the production know-how to competitors and selling them the fabric. We knew their Fuzzy Foot would sell at various prices, sizes, and qualities. The idea was simply to build as big a market as fast as we could," and, he added, "to share in it as much as we could."

To that end, Glenoit, armed with their information from Hecht's, shifted Fuzzy Foot from the rug department to the high-traffic, first-floor departments like stationery and gifts. They took Fuzzy Foot to retail outlets they'd never used before—college bookstores, supermarkets, gift shops—and distributed free rugs to private clubs, show-business types, and newspaper columnists. Art Buchwald hung some on his office wall and told visitors they were Spiro Agnew's footprints.

The result: total industry sales of almost $15 million in thirteen countries and a one-year boom for Glenoit far more profitable than what they could have achieved alone.

Like nearly every savvy promoter/manufacturer of fads, the gentlemen at Glenoit Mills used the mass media to market their fad: they gave Fuzzy Foot to the press, crossed their fingers, and banked the results. Gary Dahl of Pet Rock fame beguiled the media with wild, witty tales of individually handpicked pets; Duncan's yo-yo fad was, however unexpected, a child of the television medium. Backgammon had its very own press agent in Alexis Obolensky, Russian-born aristocrat, grand prime mover of New York's charity-ball and gossip-column crowd, and himself a fan of the game. Somewhat lonely in his enthusiasm, he took to promoting backgammon in the mid-1960's with such persistently glamor-ridden tournaments that a decade later, in 1973, the country's major manufacturer of backgammon sold as many sets as it had in the previous twenty years combined.

One of the few fads to survive an actively hostile press was skateboarding—"sidewalk surfing," as it was called in the early 1960's when it first appeared in California as an alternative to the real, wet thing. By 1965, it had national prominence, a faddish argot of its own, and several teen-age deaths to its credit. The California Medical Association branded it "the new medical menace"; Bountiful, Utah, confiscated the boards under a "public nuisance" statute, and Chattanooga, Tennessee, unearthed an old ordinance banning "any coaster toy vehicle." In Jacksonville, Florida, the charge was "impeding traffic." Wisconsin authorities enforced regulations prohibiting roller skates on public highways.

*Tina Trefethen, champ, 1976.*                    *Down-curbie end-over: all over.*

Under that kind of pressure, skateboarding receded to its original West Coast lair, where it was kept alive by an everchanging but dedicated band of the young. National resurrection came in the 1970's in the form of a tough, flexible polyurethane wheel that replaced the old wooden one and made trick skateboarding possible and relatively safe, even for novices.

By the fall of 1975, the fad had rolled back across the country to the East Coast where, in June 1976, National Skateboard Shows, Inc., invested over $250,000 to stage the Skateboard World Masters Invitational tournament in New York's suburbs. Bill Riordan, onetime manager of tennis star Jimmy Connors, was handling Ty Page by then, a teen-age star of the skateboard. "No more appearances for fifty bucks," he told his boy. "Your price is $2,500 a shot now. This is the big time, kid."

Ironically, one of the few fad products to wend its way into the big time virtually without benefit of the mass communication media was a homely, cosy variant of mass communication itself, the CB radio.

In 1958, when the FCC opened up twenty-three two-way radio channels as an alternative to the more complicated ham radio rigs, the nation's truckdrivers and a few hobbyists had the airwaves to themselves. Even among the truckers, Citizens Band

*Price (mean): 20 bucks. Sales (1976 est.): 15 million. The take: 300 million smackeroos.*

didn't take off until the Arab oil embargo gave us the 1974 energy crisis. Increasingly, the big-rig drivers used the CB to alert the brotherhood to gas stations that could sell them gas. It was so useful a means to so desirable a commodity that an estimated one million truck and automobile drivers hooked up to CB in the next eight months. Three months later, one million more licenses had been issued and an equal number of CBers had plunked down anywhere from $60 to $375 to buy the radio, but hadn't bothered to get the $4 five-year license. By then the gas shortage was over, CB was big news, and the fad spin-offs had begun: the CB bumper stickers, record albums, jacket patches, lighters, and jewelry. We can subscribe to any of several CB monthlies and tabloids, read over a dozen books on equipment, regional channel-use distribution, and "slanguage," and watch the market value of CB manufacturers' stock rise, vertically—as much as 8,000 percent in 1975.

For some women, who make up almost half of new licensees, the CB undoubtedly offers protection in the case of a midnight breakdown in the middle of a friendless nowhere. And for a good many of us CB is a mask, or so sociologist Amitai Etzioni of Columbia has suggested: "A CB allows you to present a false self. . . . Like the traveling salesman who drops into a singles bar and says he's the president of his company, a person can project on the airwaves anything he wants to be."

But above all else, what CB offers is a way of reaching out from our individual pockets of loneliness to talk to each other. There it is: a magic two-way electronic gizmo that spins friendly chatter and neighborly concern into the alienated, love-starved corners the last angry decade and a half created for us.

"Nobody," *Life* magazine said in that long-ago summer of 1955, "is mad at nobody"—thus smugly applauding a fragile moment of international peace and domestic tranquility. It would be virtually the last of those moments for years to come. Perhaps the self-satisfaction we suffered in the Fabulous Fifties made the crises that followed all the more traumatic. Traumatic they were: by 1970, "We Shall Overcome," once the rallying cry of civil rights protesters on the march, had become an alternative national anthem, a simple, resounding tune that bespoke our exhaustion with racism, sexism, ageism, the war in Vietnam, the destruction of the environment, and the droop in the dollar.

Throughout those turbulent years, as the hard hats bellowed "Our country! Right or wrong," and the flower children whispered "Love," fads showered over us like confetti, some of them born of specific crises, others born of the need to escape them all. The protest button fad blossomed in 1967, along with "personality posters" that whisked you away with Brando, Bogie, Paul Newman, and Peter Fonda, or plunged you into the maelstrom with Che, Mao, Allen Ginsburg, and Freud. One New York button manufacturer shipped out two hundred thousand buttons a month, including a batch to the folks of Prairie Village, Kansas, that called for "Jewish Power."

Even some of those who could afford to sit sublimely above the battlefield climbed down, briefly, to wallow in the mayhem. They pulled on cashmere turtlenecks and French-cut jeans and became the radically chic of 1968, haunting fund-raising parties for the Black Panthers and Cesar Chavez. Three years later, Stewart Alsop declared radical chic dead, a victim of "the winding down of the war . . . and the winding down of the U.S. economy. The latter, Alsop added, "had the sobering effect on the fashionably radical that the sight of the gallows is supposed to have on the condemned man."

SDS and the new young left made draft-card burning a major political fad in 1968, and Hermann Hesse *the* literary fad of 1969. Hesse jibed mercilessly at their favorite target—the "establishment"—and, like his readers, had little patience for that "fat and prosperous brood of mediocrity," the middle class. Smug and self-righteous, the radical young depended nevertheless on our indulgence. When John Corry, in a 1970 issue of *Harper's*, decided they were "stupefyingly dull," it signaled the beginning of the end.

More fads grew from the American Indian movement that culminated in the occupation of Wounded Knee in 1973. Throughout the following year, Navajo squash-blossom necklaces, Zuni inlay bracelets, and handmade silver and turquoise jewelry of the Southwestern tribes sprawled over the counters of Fifth Avenue merchants. More jewelry spun out of the gay-rights movement. In California during the early 1970's, a homosexual's single gold earring read "dominant" if worn in the left ear, "passive" if worn in the right. In New York a year or two later, the earring was simply kinky, no longer restricted to gays at all. Similarly, it was gays who originally wore necklaces bearing golden razor blades, created by jeweler Robin Kahn as classy tools for dividing up portions of cocaine. By 1975, they spelled neither "gay" (one was spotted at an Atlanta film premiere around the neck of Paul Newman) nor coke: New York street venders hawked them to straight tourists and their kids.

We spent a good deal of our time in the 1960's escaping, into the past and into fantasyland. James Bond was an early escape hero, his sexy competence moving 9 million books off the racks by 1970. Batman was the craze in 1966, the hottest thing on prime-time television and the inspiration for some one thousand licensed Bat-fad items—from mask-and-cape sets to Batman bubble bath—that pulled in almost $600 million. Ten years later, Spiderman ensnares millions of young kids, and the Marvel Comic Superheroes sell well in book form for the under-thirty market, four hefty volumes of them.

Monsters became a faddish escape again in the 1960's. We began reading monster comics and watching vintage monster films in 1966. By 1970, we had discovered Fuzzy Foot, the grins of our preteen "creepy boppers" were revealing fake fangs, and

*Bat boy and mentor, 1966.*

magazines like *Eerie* and *Vampirella* were attracting 2 million bloodthirsty readers annually. Aurora's line of twelve monster hobby kits sold 1.7 million styrene models in 1970 alone.

For older gore-lovers, there were "The Monster Mash," a national best-selling record, and Alice Cooper's monster music; Andy Warhol gave us a bloody *Frankenstein* and a bloodier *Dracula*. Nine hundred people showed up for a "creep chic" Halloween at Manhattan's Rainbow Room in 1974; Mel Brook's spoof *Young Frankenstein* was a box-office smasheroo in 1975; the first of the *King Kong* remakes—a $20 million dollar epic—opened in late 1976, and shot onto the all-time top-grossing film chart.

As part of our escape from "scientism," or so it's been said, we made the psychic arts faddish again. Major universities offered courses in satanism and witchcraft, 1966 sales of crystal balls in Los Angeles shot way up, and sales of Ouija boards exceeded 2.3 million in 1967, outpacing Monopoly for the first time since the real estate game appeared in 1935. Jeanne Moreau, Dick Gregory, Rosemary Harris, and Peter Sellers admitted to obtaining periodic readings, and Sellers even announced he'd consulted a clairvoyant

The Beatles, past (above) and present once more.

*Sentimental journeys. Batman (born 1939, Detective Comics No. 27) was the prime-time sensation of 1966. Even the National Safety Council applauded: This time out, Batman traveled with a safety belt. A decade later, Howdy Doody was rewigged and resuscitated for another go at the peanut gallery. And in 1977, The Beatles' golden oldies were re-released and cracking the charts once again—music to the ears of anybody who had heard the future, and preferred the past.*

annually for years. Dell Publishing sold 8 million astrological dope-sheets in 1969, and by 1972, 1,200 of the nation's 1,750 daily newspapers were carrying daily horoscopes that tracked the stars for an estimated 40 million readers.

But the greatest escape fad—for all of us—was nostalgia. The nostalgia watchers attribute it to the assassination of President Kennedy, and certainly the ransacking of the past was launched shortly thereafter. We began with the 1930's, sucking up the objects and ornaments of the Depression like a giant cultural vacuum cleaner. No matter that beneath the old comic books and the mason jars and the big-band records lay the human misery of the 1930's. "There was still adolescence in those days," said Marshall McLuhan. "And these were still remote ideals and private dreams, and visualizable goals." So we listened to broadcasts of old radio shows, bought the Superman comics, the Glenn Miller records, and the Buck Rogers ray guns once again. *Bonnie and Clyde* appeared in 1967 and *They Shoot Horses, Don't They?* in 1969, giving us back the gangsters and the marathons of the 1930's, along with the calf-length skirts and the taxi-driver caps and the Red Baron Flying Ace helmets, complete this time with

*Howdy, 1976.*

shrapnel holes. Even Frank Nitti's gangster garb came back, double-breasted, pin-striped, gaudy with palm-tree ties.

"Hollywood Camp" tested our memory for the good old lines from the bad old movies, the game itself a spin-off from the Trivia game that began at Columbia University in 1965. Trivia spawned an Ivy League Trivia Tournament, a televised hour-long "National Trivia Test," and finally made Susan Sontag's "camp" a simple umbrella word for the trivial, bizarre cultural artifacts—Big Little Books, stereoscope slides, Shirley Temple mugs, feather boas—that we had rediscovered in our need to escape the present.

"Nostalgia," said one pundit, "is where one withdraws when his emotional armor needs repairing." As the 1960's heated up, providing a distressing series of emotional shocks, we searched on for nostalgic diversion, "substitute gratification for a very real pain."

But finally, in pain and mired in protests by and/or for Blacks, gays, grays, women, and union grapes, many of us began concentrating our individual energies on that most important, most fascinating, most worthy of causes—ME.

Tom Wolfe has called the 1970's the "Me Decade," tracing its roots to the national postwar affluence that gave us what he calls "the new man, the liberated man, the first common man in the history of the world with the much dreamed-of combination of money, free time, and personal freedom." The "new man" thus began a new search—for self-mastery, self-knowledge, and the elusive goal of "realizing his potential as a human being."

One of the early discoveries of this search was "Pop Art." The movement began in the late 1950's with experimental canvases by painters like Lichtenstein and Warhol, and the first major exhibit of Pop was held at the Guggenheim Museum in 1963. This was clearly art for Wolfe's "new man," art that invited us to dwell on the symbols, objects, and memories of our own world, our own lives—art that said a Campbell's soup can is more relevant (now *there*'s a 1960's word) than a Leonardo Virgin.

By 1966, Pop had grown, said *Newsweek*, "like the Blob, from a label for what appeared to be a minor phase in art history to a mass psyche." By this time, Pop had become a prefix for "culture," embracing Batman and backless dresses, unisex and James Bond, everything camp, kitsch, nostalgic, and faddish.

*The credit card boom:*
*New money for the "new man."*

Even pure Pop Art had opened up to mass participation. Not everyone could own a Rauschenberg, but now anyone could come home with a genuine do-it-yourself-ketchup-bottle-squirt-paint-cardboard creation. And anything became art in the "happening." Early examples assaulted the senses with the simultaneous stimuli of music, film, and dance; later examples of life-as-art soared to new zeniths, sank to new nadirs of multi-faceted mayhem.

The kids caught up with the Pop Art movement by the early 1970's. For what is the graffiti-covered New York City subway system but one mammoth Pop Art kinetic sculpture. With graffiti, art for the "new man" has finally arrived at the pinnacle of relevance. Spray-paint cans in hand, our youthful artists approach a patch of virgin wall and emblazon it with that most immediate symbol of their lives—their own names.

Me. Now. That's what we're focusing on. Improving our bodies, our minds, our spirits. Self-actualizing. And doing it ourselves—with a little help from the thousands of how-to books that cram the bookstore shelves.

Tom Wolfe suggests the spirit of Me was harbingered by the Clairol ad of 1061 that said, "If I've only one life, let me live it as . . ." We've spent fifteen years filling in the blank. In San Francisco in the 1960's, an estimated three hundred thousand filled in "flower child" and looked for Me in Timothy Leary and LSD, in "acid-rock" and wire-frame glasses, in light shows and Wes Wilson's swirling, fluorescent, psychedelic posters that sold nation-wide at the rate of fifty-seven thousand a month.

Thousands of others searched at the Esalen Institute at Big Sur, where $220 a week bought self-encounter via the techniques of William Schutz and Fritz Perls. Stripping away your defenses, baring your soul, "getting in touch with yourself," you suffered the pains and humiliations happily. After all, Wolfe reminds us, "the star was *Me*."

Countless more searched for Me in the communes. By 1970, there were over two thousand communes in America, some purely secular, others basking in the charismatic light of Maharaj Ji, Maharishi Mahesh Yogi, and Swami Prabhupada, don of the Hare Krishnas. Others worshiped profane gods like Charles Manson; still others filled up with legions of the lonely and with ex-acid heads, heroine addicts, and Hell's Angels who gave everything up for Jesus. "I'll give you a free trip," said one of the saved. "It's really a groovy high. It's called Jesus Christ and it will really blow your mind." The Jesus Movement fueled a spate of fad products, from *Jesus Christ, Superstar*, a rock musical of 1971, to Jesus T-shirts, Jesus jockey shorts, Jesus bikinis, and marijuana "roach" holders shaped like crosses.

By the early 1970's we had added physical fitness to the list of goals for the complete self-actualizer. Jogging was in in 1971, and related heart-builders like cycling, swimming, even programmed walking. By 1973, Chinaphilia and Eastern religions, rising rape rates and returning Vietnam veterans fed the martial arts mania that spawned films and TV shows, and had 10 million of us grunting "Yah!" as we stalked the floor with masters of judo and jujitsu, aikido and t'ai chi, kendo, kempo, karate, and kung fu.

Today, health lies in jump rope and racquet games, and happiness is hawked by Werner Erhard and the est vanguard, by the Reverend Sun Myung Moon and his "Moonies." The Me decade moves on under a "born again" president. All will recede into history, Jimmy Carter's term limited by the laws of the land, the others by the laws of faddism.

We can speculate, but only precariously, about future fads: punk rock; more sophisticated computer games; satin boxing shorts a la Rocky; mopeds; and a fourth great roller-skating renaissance. Or perhaps we will once again be able to count on a single fad to keep tabs on the rest. In 1976 and the first months of 1977 we had "Mary Hartman, Mary Hartman," a television soap opera spoof that served, said *The New York Times*, as a "cultural signpost." Mary took on country music, est, sex therapy, CB radios, and even the Bo and Peep freaks who still await the UFO that will spirit them to wherever.

Millions of us watched Mary Hartman as she stumbled through her Fernwood kitchen, and her life. And she watched right back. A University of California course explained that the folks of Fernwood reflected "the dreams and nightmares of the American people." Indeed, for the moment, we were the folks of Fernwood. And they, like all our fads, were us.

*The folks of Fernwood, signposts of their times.*

*Beatlemania at Buckingham Palace, 1966. "We're more popular than Jesus," John Lennon crowed that summer. Not everyone agreed (see, for example, opposite).*

# HIGH, HIGHER, HIGHEST:
## MIND AND BODY IN THE SIXTIES AND SEVENTIES

From The Beatles to the Reverend Moon, a portfolio of the trips we've taken in the last decade and a half.

Moonmania. Above, the Reverend Sun Myung Moon, self-proclaimed Messiah of the masses. At left, the symbol of his Unification Church—claiming, as of 1976, over thirty-thousand followers among the young, who each year hustle up an estimated $10 million for the coffers of their cult.

Jesus Freaks erupt in protest, Candlestick Park, San Francisco, 1966.

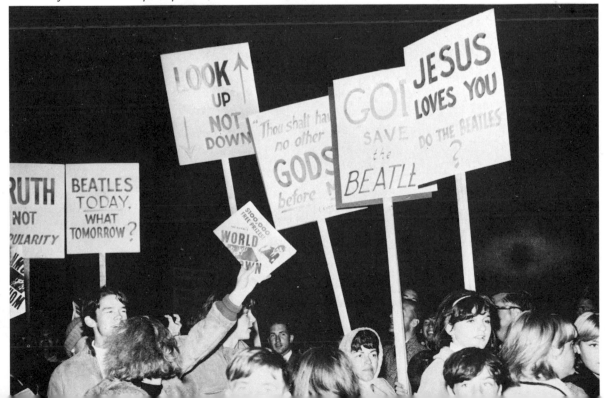

High on Krishna, San Francisco, 1974.

Higher, New York City, 1975.

*Getting a rise out of the trampoline craze, 1961.*

*Piano-wrecking, chop-chop, 1974.*

*Seventy-two above, twin bed below, Southeastern Oklahoma State, 1961.*

*Kissathon, Fort Lauderdale, Spring 1974.*

*Getting it together for a dance marathon, Syracuse U., 1973.*

*Freaking on Frisbees. Above left and right, World Frisbee Championships, Michigan, 1976; below, a Midwest tournament, 1969.*

Skateboarding, the second time around. Above and below
right, coasting styles on a New York City street, 1976;
below left, Russ Howell, all-time freestyle champion, 1976.

*A seventy-eight-year-old Mandarin, second from right, leads devotees
in T'ai Chi exercises at dawn, San Francisco's Chinatown, 1972.*

*Hang-gliding near Pine Mountain, Oregon, 1973.*

*Kansas City joggers, 1967.*

*Some of the two-hundred buttocks attending a Memphis State streak, March 1974.*

*Two Berkeley students, above, don wigs
in an unsuccessful attempt to disguise their sex.*

*"Peace in our time."* A Midwest street corner, 1974.

# Picture Credits

All pictures, except those listed below, are from the archives of Wide World Photos, New York.

## BEGINNINGS

2, left, private collection. 3, private collection. 4, above, New York Public Library Picture Collection; below, private collection. 5, above and below left, courtesy of Parker Brothers; center right, courtesy of Wham-O Manufacturing; bottom right, courtesy of Selchow & Righter Company. 6, above, New York Public Library Picture Collection; below, private collection. 7, courtesy of Wham-O Manufacturing. 8, New York Public Library Picture Collection. 9, above left and below right, New York Public Library Picture Collection. 10–11, New York Public Library Picture Collection. 12, New York Public Library Picture Collection. 18, New York Public Library Picture Collection. 19, private collection. 20, above, private collection. 22, New York Public Library Picture Collection. 23, left, private collection; above right, from the Greenway Production for ABC-TV. 24, New York Public Library Picture Collection. 25, top, New York Public Library Picture Collection; bottom, courtesy of Parker Brothers. 26–27, all, courtesy of Parker Brothers. 28, below, courtesy of Parker Brothers.

## "YES, WE HAVE NO BANANAS"

34, courtesy of Foote Cone & Belding. 38, courtesy of Foote Cone & Belding. 45, above, private collection. 46–47, New York Public Library Picture Collection. 50, bottom, JoAnne Day, "Decorative Silhouettes of the Twenties for Designers and Craftsmen," Dover Publications. 51, left and above right, private collections.

## "BROTHER, CAN YOU SPARE A DIME?"

76, courtesy of Foote Cone & Belding. 78, private collection. 80, courtesy of Foote Cone & Belding. 82, below right, courtesy of Foote Cone & Belding. 84, left, NBC Photo; center left and right, and bottom right, courtesy of Foote Cone & Belding. 85, courtesy of Foote Cone & Belding. 87, above right, courtesy of Parker Brothers. 89, above, courtesy of Foote Cone & Belding. 90, above, private collection; below, courtesy of CBS. 91, right, courtesy of CBS. 94, below right, private collection. 96, top left, private collection.

## "IT'S HOWDY DOODY TIME!"

99, courtesy of Buffalo Bob Enterprises, 103, courtesy of Foote Cone & Belding. 107, private collection. 117, center and bottom, private collections.125, above, private collection. 127, above, private collection. 131, above right, courtesy of Foote Cone & Belding. 133, below, courtesy of Wham-O Manufacturing.

## "WE SHALL OVERCOME"

154–155, all, Christina Birrer. 158, from the Greenway Production for ABC-TV. 159, courtesy of CBS. 160, courtesy of Foote Cone & Belding. 163, courtesy of T.A.T. Communications. 170, all, courtesy of Wham-O Manufacturing. 171, all, courtesy of Christina Birrer.

# Select Bibliography

*Books and Essays*

The following are of general interest within their categories. Books on specific fads have not been listed.

FAD THEORY

Blumer, Herbert G. "Fashion," *International Encyclopedia of the Social Sciences*. New York: Macmillan, 1968.

Katz, Elihu, and Lazarsfeld, Paul F. *Personal Influence*. Glencoe, Illinois: Free Press, 1956.

Kracke, Don, with Honkanen, Roger. *How to Turn Your Idea Into a Million Dollars*. Garden City, N.Y.: Doubleday, 1977.

Meyersohn, Rolf, and Katz, Elihu. "Notes on a Natural History of Fads," in *Mass Leisure*, edited by Eric Larrabee and Rolf Meyersohn. Glencoe, Illinois: Free Press, 1958.

Reisman, David. *The Lonely Crowd*, Abr. ed. New Haven, Conn.: Yale University Press, 1969.

Rosenberg, Bernard, and White, David M., eds. *Mass Culture*. Glencoe, Illinois: Free Press, 1957.

Sapir, Edward. "Fashion," *Encyclopedia of the Social Sciences*, vol. III. New York: Macmillan, 1937.

Turner, Ralph, and Killian, Lewis, eds. *Collective Behavior*. Englewood Cliffs: Prentice-Hall, 1957.

Popular Culture

*Best of Life.* New York: Time-Life Books, 1973.

Griffith, Richard, and Mayer, Arthur. *The Movies.* New York: Simon & Schuster, 1957.

Lynes, Russell. *The Tastemakers.* New York: Harper & Bros., 1955.

McWhirter, Norris, and McWhirter, Ross. *The Guiness Book of World Records.* 1976 ed. New York: Bantam, 1976.

Nye, Russell. *The Unembarrassed Muse.* New York: Dial Press, 1970.

Phelps, Robert, and Deane, Peter. *The Literary Life.* New York: Farrar, Straus & Giroux, 1968.

Ross, Ishbel. *Taste in America.* New York: Thomas Y. Crowell Company, 1967.

Sann, Paul. *Fads, Follies and Delusions of the American People.* New York: Crown, 1967.

Wallechinsky, David, and Wallace, Irving. *The People's Almanac.* Garden City, N.Y.: Doubleday, 1975.

White, David M., ed. *Pop Culture in America.* New York: New York Times Book Ser., 1970.

Historical Background

Bird, Caroline. *The Invisible Scar.* New York: David McKay, 1966.

Sklar, Robert, ed. *The Plastic Age: 1917–1930.* New York: Braziller, 1970.

Stevenson, Elizabeth. *The American 1920s; Babbitts & Bohemians.* New York: Macmillan, 1967.

*This Fabulous Century*, vols. I-VIII. New York: Time-Life Books, 1969–1971.

## Articles

The following listings include articles of general interest for the study of fads. While articles on specific fads are not included, the reader should note that *Reader's Guide to Periodical Literature* uses "Fads," "Food Fads," and "College Student Fads" as subject headings. *The Journal of Sociology* and *Sociological*

*Quarterly* frequently contain articles on relevant matters. Popular magazines with extensive coverage of fad phenomena have included *Look* (in the early 1960s), and *Life* (from the late 1950's until its demise); *Seventeen* included a monthly review of teen-age fads in its "Teen Scene" column, from 1965–1969; and the most reliable sources for modern fad-watchers remain *Time* (since the early 1960's) and *Newsweek* (from the late 1950's).

### Fad Theory

Bogardus, Emory S. "Social Psychology of Fads," *Journal of Applied Sociology* 8 (1924): 234–43.

Janney, J. E. "Fad and Fashion Leadership Among Undergraduate Women," *Journal of Abnormal Psychology* 36 (1941): 275–78.

Simmel, Georg. "Fashion," *American Journal of Sociology* 62 (1957): 541–58 (originally published in 1904).

Soldan, F. L. "What Is a Fad?" *National Education Association Journal of Addresses and Proceedings 1901:* 85–94.

"Time to Talk of Fads and Fruit Flys." *Business Week*, 28 August 1971, p. 70.

### Fads in Historical Context

Benchley, P. "Story of Pop," *Newsweek* 67, 25 April 1966, p. 56.

Chaze, Elliot. "March of Mad Fads," *Life* 49, 26 December 1960, p. 110.

"Cool Facts about Teen-age Fads," *Womans Home Companion* 83, July 1956, p. 53.

"Fads of the Fifties," *Look* 24, 2 February 1960, pp. 83–8.

"Follies That Come with Spring," *Time* 89, 24 March 1967, pp. 52–3.

Griswold, W. S. "Can You Invent a Million Dollar Fad?" *Popular Science* 188, January 1966, p. 78.

Grove, A. "On Fads," *Cornhill Magazine* 81, April 1900, pp. 515–23.

Laird, D. A. "Have You a Fad?" *Review of Reviews* 91, March 1925, pp. 31–4.

Meehan, Thomas. "Must We Be Nostalgic about the Fifties?" *Horizon* 9, Winter 1972, p. 10.

"Nostalgia," *Newsweek* 76, 28 December 1970, pp. 34–8.

"On Faddists," *Living Age* 265, 25 June 1910, pp. 817–19.

Ray, B. "The Nifty Fifties," *Life* 72, 16 June 1972, pp. 38–46.

Smith, R. P. "Through Darkest Middle Age with Fading Memory," *Good Housekeeping* 148, April 1959, p. 69.

Steinem, Gloria. "Ins and Outs of Pop Culture," *Life* 59, 20 August 1965, p. 72.

"Teenage Fads; Groovy or Uptight?" *Senior Scholastic* 92, 25 April 1968, pp. 12–13.

Townsend, R. T. "Fads and Fancies," *Country Life in America* 52, October 1927, p. 47.

Waters, H. F. "The Teen-agers: Rites, Styles, Passwords," *Newsweek* 67, 21 March 1966, pp. 74–5.

Weichsel, H. S., M.D. "Fashions in Medicine," *Harper's Magazine* 219, November 1959, pp. 69–74.

Wolfe, Tom. "The Me Decade," *New York*, 23 August 1976, pp. 26–40.

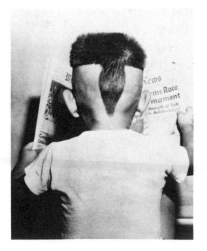

## DATE DUE

| | | | |
|---|---|---|---|
| FEB 5 '80 | | | |
| OC 27 '82 | | | |
| FEB 8 1984 | | | |
| FEB 28 1984 | | | |
| MAY 14 1984 | | | |
| | | | |
| | | | |
| | | | |
| | | | |
| | | | |
| | | | |
| | | | |
| | | | |
| | | | |